LOS GATOS PUBLIC LIBRARY

D1161343

THE LAST OF THE WALLENDAS

THE LAST OF THE WALLENDAS

Delilah Wallenda
and
Nan DeVincentis-Hayes

NEW HORIZON PRESS
Far Hills, New Jersey

Library of Congress Catalog Card Number: 92-60564 /24

Delilah Wallenda and Nan DeVincentis-Hayes
  The Last of the Wallendas

ISBN: 0-88282-116-4
New Horizon Press

1997 1996 1995 1994 1993 / 5 4 3 2 1
Manufactured in the U.S.A.

210630

We dedicate this to our families who have patiently stood by us while we diligently worked on this book. We thank them, too, for the time and energies they have put into helping us in this endeavor. We are eternally grateful.

Our love to our husbands, Terry Troffer and Jim Hayes, and to our children: Nikolas and Lijana Troffer, and Marta and Brynne Hayes.

WALLENDA FAMILY TREE—DAUGHTER JENNY

Karl Wallenda ⊤ Martha Schepp
Jenny

Jenny ⊤ Alberto Zoppe

Olinka ⊤ Tino   Delilah ⊤ Terry Troffer

Alida Andrea Aurelia Alex   Lijana Nikolas

Jenny ⊣⊢ Dick Faughan

Jenny ⊤ Andy Anderson
Tammy

Erica   Blake

WALLENDA FAMILY TREE—DAUGHTER CARLA

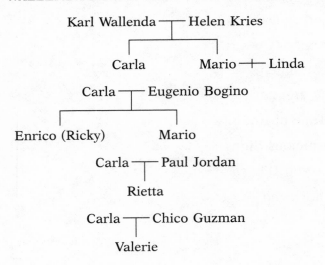

Karl Wallenda ⊤ Helen Kries

Carla   Mario ⊣⊢ Linda

Carla ⊤ Eugenio Bogino

Enrico (Ricky)   Mario

Carla ⊤ Paul Jordan
Rietta

Carla ⊤ Chico Guzman
Valerie

CONTENTS

And indeed there will be time
To wonder, "Do I dare?" and,
"Do I dare?"

—T.S. Eliot
The Love Song of J. Alfred Prufrock

ACKNOWLEDGMENTS

Our thanks to Jenny Wallenda, Mario and Linda Wallenda, Gunther and Sheila Wallenda, and all those who gave us their time and permission in interviewing them, including Evelyn Fossett, Debbie Goetsch, and Manfred Duvall.

And thanks to Ron Morris, author of *Karl Wallenda*, for all his help, cooperation, and for allowing us the use of his book.

Authors' Note

These are the actual experiences and history of Delilah Wallenda, and this book reflects her opinion of the past, present, and future. The personalities, events, actions, and conversations portrayed within the story have been reconstructed from her memory, extensive interviews, and research, utilizing court documents, letters, personal papers, press accounts, and the memories of participants. In an effort to safeguard the privacy of certain individuals, the authors have changed their names and, in some cases, altered otherwise identifying characteristics. Events involving the characters happened as described; only minor details have been altered.

PROLOGUE

She looks up. Strung against the electric blue sky, the highwire glitters. High in the heavens, the long narrow ladder seems to touch the clouds and sways back and forth.

She steps on the first rung of the ladder. Then the next and the next after that until finally she's on the top step and then on the platform.

Up there, the wind is ferocious. It beats at her face and blows her long chestnut hair in her eyes. She shivers. Her breaths come quick and shallow.

Before stepping out on the shiny sliver of steel, she glances down. Under her, the spectators look no bigger than toothpicks and the cars no bigger than toy models.

She stands perfectly still for a moment wanting to sense the direction of the wind, the direction of her life and, as she always does, she closes her eyes to ask for God's blessing.

Then she's ready. She takes a step out on the metal wire, perceives it vibrating, and casts a glance down the wire—it's a long journey across that thin filament to the other side, but like all the other skywalks she's done, she gathers her courage to walk this one, too.

Below her the crowd whistles, claps, stamps, encourages her to go on.

The wind buffets her small frame atop the wire. A dark thought crosses her mind. On another windy day like this one, her grandfather died. He tumbled off the wire, which was stretched to one hundred feet, and plummeted to his death. Today the wire is stretched to four hundred feet. There is no net beneath her just as there was none beneath him. She knows that what happened to him could just as easily happen to her. He, after all, was Karl Wallenda, the most famous highwire artist of all time. She had thought about his fall endless times and has even in her own way prepared for her own. However, she won't allow fear, danger, or tragedy to prevent her from going on.

Now, like the true performer she is, she smiles and waves to the audience. Slowly, elegantly, she places one foot in front of the other, with each squared precisely on the steel line until she reaches the middle of the wire. Then she executes a split and a salute with absolute precision. Her graceful movements make her look like a ballerina gliding around the stage on point instead of a daredevil taking her life in her hands as she inches across a skinny cable high above the ground.

She walks on. She has reached the three-quarter mark now. Not far away is the other platform where she can step off and work her way back down to safety, security.

She takes a deep breath, knowing she cannot afford overconfidence. Even the few paces left to the platform are dangerous. It only takes one slip. One wrong move to catapult into disaster. Nevertheless, if she thinks about that too long —that the earth lies far below her and its hardness could be her demise—she will lose concentration . . . and with it her life. No, she must hold her feelings in check and continue to walk on whether the distance is short or long, whether conditions are windy or calm, whether she's ill or well, or whether her life is filled with joy or despair.

For she is one of the last Wallendas. The circus is her life. The wire is her calling, her mission.

ONE

The Circus Is Dying

Silhouetted through the window, the darkening sky is streaked with pink. It is twilight. Delilah Wallenda and her husband Terry Troffer sit with some other circus performers inside her modest L-shaped ranch home in Sarasota. Occasionally Delilah glances outside to the wire strung from one palm tree to another in the back yard. Next door to Delilah is her brother Tino, and not too far away are her mother and the winter headquarters of all the Wallendas. Her focus shifts back to the anxious faces in the room. They are waiting for the telephone to ring. It is silent.[1]

"Bookings are trickling in much too slowly," Delilah sighs.

"I hate this time of year," Terry says wearily. The others nod in agreement.

For them April is indeed the cruelest month. While the world seems to be gearing up for the coming spring, the circus performers are gearing down for the worst year ever.

"Few, if any, job commitments for the summer have come in," Terry injects. "This bides bad news; no offers now means no work later in what is usually our busy season."

"I don't know if we can hold out till then. We have awfully slim reserves," Delilah wistfully adds.

"How's none," another voice pipes up. "The issue is no longer one of how profitable the summer will be but if we'll survive the season."

"This year is no better than last and in some ways it's even worse." Delilah glances at her husband worriedly.

"I know," Terry grows angry, moody. "What once was a profitable and enjoyable lifestyle has now become a nightmare. Circuses unfortunately are dying out in today's high-tech, fast-paced world where many people prefer to sit at home in a La-Z-Boy and watch television rather than make the effort to get dressed and drive to a live performance; this is another reason for the demise of the business."

Ron Morris, author and circus concessionaire, shakes his head. "I've been in circuses all my life, and I've never seen it as bad as it is today. Live entertainment will never again be the same. Electronics are the culprit; they cause laziness in consumers who'd rather stay home and watch television or play electronic games. Because of costs, bit troupes, like Karl's, will no longer be in existence."

Evie Fossett, who does the sway pole and revolving moon acts and is known in the business as Miss Evelyn, agrees, "Circuses are dying. The promoters aren't interested in purchasing and boosting the good acts—all they want is to sell the concessions. They don't care what your act is, how you do it, or how much talent and practice it takes. They just want you to be cheap. Veterans like us only get called if promoters can't find the inexpensive and inferior acts. And to get any work, you have to be willing to travel all over America and to other countries. It's not a promising future."

Debbie Goetsch, a seventeen-year veteran who does a juggling gaucho act while her husband walks the tightwire, leans back in her chair and adds, "Producers keep trying to underbid each other, so no one ends up with a quality act. As a result, many foreigners get hired because they're willing to work for nothing just to get into the States. Quality professionals are offered the same money beginners get, so why should pros spend all that time trying to improve their act or even risk their lives if they're not appreciated? Producers sell audiences short, thinking spectators won't care what the quality of the act is or who the performers are, but I think spectators do care but just don't complain about it. A secret to staying alive in the business is to find outlets other than circuses. My husband and I are going the route of working cruise ships, which we enjoy because the pay and hours are good, and our overhead is almost nil. But in spite of the problems, I wouldn't change my lifestyle for a second. I'm a performer, an artist, and like all artists, I do what I do because I have to."

Manfred Duvall, a veteran of both American and European circuses, brings up still another concern. "American circuses, unlike their overseas counterparts, are hurting. In other countries the artists don't have the pressures that American performers do. For instance, the Russian state used to pay a salary to all their show people, plus expenses: traveling costs, costumes, living accommodations on the road and at home, cars, equipment, everything. Even the cost of hiring engineers to transport and set up the rigging was paid for by the state. But here in the United States, performers have to pay for everything themselves. That's the reason foreign performers are making it and American showmen aren't. It's the same reason circuses are dying in the States. Something has to be done."[2]

Duvall spills over with stories about his experiences performing in Russia and other countries, such as the time he was on a cultural exchange program with the USSR where he was given a third-class hotel with no toilets, while Rus-

3

sians in America received the royal treatment. He adds, "In Russia, many people are starving, and yet its one hundred circuses, as well as its gymnastics schools and other institutions for training future circus performers, receive support. They even sponsor caretakers and vets on bear farms. But here in the United States, it's all a trainer can do to maintain his animals, and costs to keep them—feed, transport, maintain their health—borders on a fortune. Worse, the animal protection people in the States protest the use of wild animals as circus performers, so many trainers lose their animals and thus their income." Duvall sums up in his thick accent: "America, our big, rich country, allows its artists to starve, die out."

Everyone in the room nods. Delilah, too, sadly shakes her head, while again looking at the cable suspended outside. Manfred's words shake her, for she understands the circus's future is in jeopardy.

"What will I do?" asks Delilah. "My life has always been intertwined with what it means to be a famous Wallenda. I walk the wire because it's in my blood. It's what I do and what my mother Jenny and grandfather Karl did before me. Those who care as much as I do, must fight. The circus tradition is in its last frontier, but I won't give up. I have to preserve our heritage and our future."

TWO

The Family Tree

Delilah Wallenda's roots are deeply embedded in circus tradition. Her forefathers were jugglers, tumblers, and street itinerants.[3]

Although the Wallendas proclaim German ancestry, their lineage really began in a Bavarian Bohemian town that, through shifting European borders, came under the rule of Germany. As circuses became prominent in Europe, the Wallendas learned a variety of art forms in order to make a living in the business. They performed as robots, trapeze artists, dancers, and slackwire artists and trained a variety of animals, from Great Danes to seals, lions, and wolves.

Delilah's history is filled with great-great-grandfathers, great-great-grandmothers, great-great-uncles, and great-aunts who served in the circus. The Wallendas raised their children to become performers. The precedent was set by Johannes Wallenda, who was a master acrobat. His son, Karl the first, ran an arena while Karl's wife entertained with a seal act. Delilah's mother was the noted highwire artist Jenny Wallenda, but most famous of all, of course, was her grandfather, the man who trained Delilah—Karl Wallenda. Delilah says, "Everybody loved Vati, but he was strict when it came to training us to become circus performers. Then he was like a slave driver, always demanding from us perfection and absolute discipline to the art."

Karl Wallenda's name is still synonymous with the word "circus." As the most famous highwire walker who ever lived, he lived a life of which others only dream—a life filled with daring achievements, danger, and excitement. Moreover, he left the world a legacy of faith and courage.

But Karl's history, entangled in affairs, divorces, remarriages, and a tumultus circus life, reads like a hot, steamy novel.

Karl (referred to as "Karl the second" here) was born the second child of Englebert Wallenda and Kunigunde Jameson. Herman, the first child, was four years old, while Willie, the last child, was a year younger. Their mother, Kunigunde, had a tumultuous history herself, having had an Irish-whiskey drinking father who ended up disgracing his entire family, especially Kunigunde's mother. Karl's father, Englebert, was the only son born to Karl the first. Like the Wallendas before him, Karl the second took his place as a show-child in the newly turned twentieth-century, fifth-generation circus family. Karl's grandfather, Karl the first, ran an arena while his grandmother, Elsie, entertained with a seal act. Johannes had been the master acrobat who set the precedent for the rest of the family. His father was a flying trapezist and a sometimes-clown. From all this came Karl's romance with the circus and his love affair with the highwire.

Some claim that Karl's grandchildren—the Wallendas who perform today—are the eleventh generation of circus Wallendas; others assert they are only the sixth generation. Delilah was born into this generation, which still performs in circuses, and a few of this group who have children— Karl's great-grandchildren—are beginning to train on the wire. Most claim, though, that it will be unlikely, with most circuses in dire economic straits, for an eighth generation of Wallenda circus folks to exist.

The early twentieth century was a difficult time. While primitive health conditions gave rise to the deadly diphtheria bacteria, primitive emotions brought to the surface by hardship and poverty made for a difficult family life. This seemed especially true for the Wallendas. Karl like to give his father the benefit of the doubt by saying that Englebert's bad temper and infidelity were attributable to those years of illness and struggles, but in reality he knew his father was a mean man. Delilah Wallenda, Karl's granddaughter, offers, "Like my grandfather, I would like to think Great-grandfather Englebert was just a victim of the times, but down deep I realize he was just plain nasty. He beat my grandfather and walked out on his family."

Englebert's temper seems to have been widely known, as he seldom made an attempt to hide it. Karl described one incident as particularly traumatic for him. His father owned a small arena—a place that Karl loved to play in. Biding his time in the office wagon was another favorite activity, so he'd go into the wagon and entertain himself. He had been only four when Englebert came upon him in the office, playing with a stack of business papers that he, like any small child, managed to scatter all over the floor. Incensed with his son's carelessness, Englebert picked Karl up and hurled him through the rear door of the wagon, yelling and cursing all the while. Karl landed hard on his right side, damaging the nerves and tissues in his ear. He never regained hearing in that ear, and what little relationship Karl had with his father vanished that day.

Like Karl, Mama Kunigunde Wallenda had felt the brunt of Englebert's temper. She did her best to keep peace in the house so that her husband would not abuse her and the children, but when she caught him having an affair with the family maid, she ended their marriage. They divorced shortly after, in 1911, and Englebert's ménage à trois became public. Stories abound about what actually happened to Karl's father through the years. Supposedly he remained a catcher in his trapeze act until he turned sixty. After that, no one is sure, but one story has him joining an African safari.

Husbandless, Mama did the best she could with her brood, but she ended up having to put six-year-old Karl and his younger brother Willy in a Catholic orphanage for a year while Karl's older brother, Herman, then ten, stayed with Mama Wallenda to work. To bring in money, Mama and Herman traveled with her mother's vaudeville business. At the end of their first year in the orphanage, Karl was sent back to live with Mama while Willy was made to live with his father Englebert, who incorporated Willy into his flying trapeze act.

Circuses in those years seldom stayed in one place; instead, they moved from town to town, setting up wherever they could get a permit to put on a show. Karl said that he attended over 160 different schools where he often was picked on by other kids. And if he wasn't in some fight, he sat in the classroom drawing pictures of circus life. Being in the circus always meant suffering the "new kid on the block" syndrome. Because traveling circuses moved by wagon in those days, he and his family were often confused with gypsies, which did not help his image at any new school. At age seven, Karl struggled to bring in money to help feed his mother and siblings. He ended up doing handstands on wobbling chairs and church steeples as a way to make money. He also entertained in beer gardens, when he was barely old enough to attend first grade. After such performances, he would "pass the hat" and watch as drinkers tossed coins into it; this was a major source of income for his family. Karl became adept at knowing what nights would be good ones and what nights would give him barely enough to feed himself and his family. In order to keep his acts fresh as he traveled from beer garden to beer garden, he constantly devised new acts or variations. He soon came to understand that variety in acts—especially daredevil ones— pleased crowds who were then more willing to part with a ruble or two and he needed this extra money badly. It allowed him to buy heating coal to warm his family on those frigid nights, although he often said a night of a hundred handstands at twenty or more beer gardens sometimes paid less than what a chunk of coal cost. Reflecting on his past to many including his granddaughter, Delilah, Karl said years later, "I don't know exactly when it was I changed from being a boy to a man."

Two years with her mother's circus were enough for Mama Wallenda. She quit and remarried, again to a circus performer. Her new husband, George Grotefant, was sixteen years younger than she and only ten years older than her son Herman. George had never been married before and wanted children. With him a whole new family was born.

From 1911 to 1916, the Wallendas endured hardships, especially during the war years, and Karl, it seemed, took the brunt of them. By 1915 George had served a year in the army, where he played coronet in the band, leaving Karl to again become the breadwinner at age ten; Herman, in the meanwhile, was living in a hotel elsewhere where he worked on an assembly line making munitions. Karl was not only responsible for himself and Willy, but now he had half-siblings—Arthur, four, and Gertrude, five—to take care of.

The year 1916 brought even greater tragedy. Hulde, a sweet cherubim of a baby, was born healthy only to soon contact diphtheria. Mama Kunigunde was near hysteria seeing her infant fading away, and on the night that Hulde's condition worsened, Karl rushed her to the hospital, running as fast as he could through freezing temperatures. The snow was a foot deep. He held the baby in his arms, close to his chest, hoping his body heat would keep her warm. He later told of the doom that enshrouded him as he nestled his baby sister against him, feeling the intense warmth from her burning his skin. She died in his arms.

However, life seemed to become a little better when George returned from the service and Herman returned from the munitions assembly line. The family decided, in spite of rough times, to set up their own circus, one they christened "Circus Wallenda."

"Circus Wallenda" consisted of Karl, 15, Herman, 19, George, 29, and Mama Kunigunde, who was around 45 years old at the time. Needing another hand, the Wallendas-Grotefants took on a fifth person—Lucie Marks, 19. The entire trope was multi-talented, performing theatrical sketches, circus tricks, and outlandish physical contortions, as well as setting up a band, with George playing the trumpet, Herman the tenor horn, and Karl on the drums. Perhaps because of his deafness in one ear or simply because he had the musical talent of a moose, the troupe, who loved Karl dearly, did all they could to out-maneuver his playing anything resembling music. Even though George Grotefant, Mama's new spouse, was not Karl's real father, he treated Mama's children as though they were his own. Karl described George as jolly, congenial, and an all-around circus artist and fixer-upper, a nice guy who couldn't for the life of him run a business with the help of ten elves, let alone by himself.

The Wallenda-Grotefant circus moved from town to town, staying wherever they were when the money ran out. From there, the men went elsewhere in search of other jobs. Often they bided their time by performing as clowns, or fill-ins—anything that would earn them some income. Sometimes, however, no circus work was available. Then drastic steps had to be taken to keep the family from starving. Karl ended up working in a coal mine until another circus booking came along; he despised every second he worked there.

During 1921, another difficult economic period, Karl and his family were again looking for jobs. He happened across a newspaper ad calling for someone who could do handstands. To him, this was a snap; he, after all, had gained experience doing handstands in beer gardens. Better still, this was *circus work*, meaning no more coal mines. Almost immediately he was en route to the city of Breslau to meet the man who put the advertisement in the paper.

The man who ran the ad, Louis Weitzman, was a huge, stubbly-faced, fortyish curmudgeon. The introductions were made and Weitzman, a cigar hanging from his mouth, looked at Karl and announced, "I want someone who can do a handstand."

Karl felt elated, but what Weitzman went on to say made Karl's heart palpitate.

"Not just any handstand," Weitzman added. "But one done on a highwire, on top of my feet while I do a handstand on the wire, sixty feet high in the air."

Karl's mouth flew open. The man had to be nuts! Surely

no one had ever survived such a suicidal mission! Weitzman was insistent that it could be done, and Karl was just as insistent that it couldn't, but he finally decided to try, knowing that the family needed money so badly.

Describing the first time he went up on the highwire, Karl said, "I put my hand on Weitzman's shoulder and followed him out on the wire to somewhere in the middle. Then he did a headstand on the wire and I climbed on him to do a handstand on his feet."

After that Karl spent endless hours and weeks crossing a cable with a pole in his hand and Weitzman's voice in his good ear barking orders: "How many times must I tell you to get that pole higher!" or "Set your feet down harder on the wire!" and "Practice, Wallenda, practice!" In the end, Karl was the only person who successfully could do the trick, not only in Breslau but elsewhere with a wire strung across rivers, between buildings and over wide spans—anywhere Weitzman could think of that was a challenge with a kamikaze flavor.

This was the beginning of Karl's career as a skywalker.

Even with steady employment, Karl suffered from poverty, unable to afford his own room or buy himself something to eat other than *wurst tzibble*, a cheap type of German baloney. He had been reduced to eating so much of it that he swore that when he got a regular, sound-paying job, he would never touch the stuff again. To that end, Karl understood that he had to remain with Weitzman. He did his best to get along with Weitzman while learning the trade.

However, all was not smooth-running. The German impresario, who had just been released from a labor camp, was a gruff slave driver. In his act was a nineteen-year-old female performer named Margarita to whom Weitzman was especially insensitive and uncaring. Although he was sorry for her, Karl knew enough to keep his distance so that he wouldn't incur Weitzman's rage. However, Margarita was attracted to him and found ways to get him to notice her, setting up little traps for him to fall into. The naive Karl went stumbling into every one of them.

One morning when Weitzman wasn't around and Margarita knew Karl would appear as usual for breakfast, she donned a see-through cotton dress and opened the top buttons. She flirted and teased Karl with her stunning figure and flowing hair until Karl asked, "How about a little kiss, Margarita?" Margarita lifted her dress inches above her hips and went over and stood before Karl. Karl's chest thumped rapidly. But then Margarita broke into sobs and, pointing to her hips, cried, "Weitzman bit me! What are you going to do about it?"

Karl protested, saying he didn't want to get involved, didn't want to irk Weitzman and lose his job. He tried to leave, but Margarita leaped at him, hissing and kicking, pounding her fists on his chest. They were interrupted by Weitzman.

Not long after, when Weitzman was balancing Karl upside down on his feet, he snarled, "Listen, stay away from Margarita. If I see you talk to her just once, I'll shake you off the wire!" Eventually Weitzman let him alone, but the rift between the two men grew wide and deep.

It was around this time that Karl came across Princess Magneta—a theatrical act in the circus in which a presumably talented magician appeared to cause a young woman to levitate. Karl was attracted to the blond girl who seemed vulnerable, so he walked over to her. Feeling Karl's sympathy, she unburdened herself, telling Karl that her magician-boss was a slave driver and that she was unhappy. She explained who she was—Magdalena Schmidt—and that she was twenty-six, ten years older than Karl, and very lonely and depressed. Karl, who called her Lena, took her on walks in secluded spots, listened to her, and found both a friend and a mother in her. It was on one of these walks, hidden away from the barkers barking, people walking and talking, and cruel bosses ordering them around, that Lena indoctrinated Karl into manhood. It was his first experience. From then on, they secretly met whenever they could.

During this time, Karl noticed Margarita's expanding waistline, as had Weitzman. Unhappy with her pregnant condition, Weitzman made her take a leave from the act. He turned to Karl and asked: "What about that Magdalena friend of yours as a replacement?" Karl thought about it. Lena continued to hate her boss, so why not ask her? Lena willingly gave up her role as Princess Magneta and joined Weitzman and Karl in their act.

Lena proved herself competent on the wire and all seemed to be going well, but brooding behind the scenes Margarita had become angry and jealous of her replacement. She began badgering both Karl and Lena, day in and day out, until it became outright harassment. Finally, Karl and Lena quit the Weitzman troupe.

The years 1923–32 brought excitement and challenges to Karl, as well as the sweet taste of love. Having lived apart for a short while in order to find jobs, he and Lena returned to each other to tour Germany, Austria, and Italy with the Strassburger Circus, in which Karl had his own highwire act. Lena performed on the highpole—an act in which she'd climb atop a lofty flexible pole and perform tricks, then slide down it in a "slide-for-life" style. At this time, a chap named Joe Geiger joined Karl's act, and the three became notable as highwire performers. Geiger stayed with Karl until 1949. Part of the thrill for Karl was performing without a net—a habit that would cost him dearly later in life—but this time Strassburger Circus mandated he have one. Having no money, he had to go to his father to beg for help in buying the net. His father responded by humiliating Karl. Worse, when the old man finally relented and loaned him some money at 20 percent interest, Karl had to accept his father's terms. The only good to have come out of that trip was Karl getting to see his brother Willy. In the meantime, Karl's other brother, Herman, had left his job in Halle, Germany, to join Karl.

Having learned from Weitzman the value of topping an act, so that the next performance would be even more daring and spectacular, Karl took to theatrics, wearing costumes, especially the nautical suits that became the Wallenda trademark. He fired blanks from a pistol into the air while standing on a bar slung between Joe and Herman. In answer to every act that competed with his, Karl came up with another stunt even more outrageous than the last. He performed each one on the highwire. However, the three-piece, heavy wooden balancing poles were always a consideration in creating new stunts. It was during this time that Herman, whose mind had a mathematical bent, invented the light-weight, one-piece, tubular steel balancing pole. It was also at this time that George, Karl's stepfather, suggested they form another circus of their own, this one to be called "The Wallenda Circus." Their repertoire consisted of the highwire, highpole, revolving ladder, Lena's slide-for-life, Joe Geiger's Houdini and juggling acts, George and Herman's comedy routines, Karl's chair-stands, and a variety of other stunts and theatrical scripts.

Nevertheless, the Wallenda Circus was doomed from the start; permits to perform in various locales were hard to obtain, and costs spiraled upward. Increasing the number of the troupe meant more money for salaries, housing for the

crew, and additional overhead. Desperate for money between engagements, Karl signed up the troupe to work for
other circuses. One such work-for-hire was the Busch Circus, in which Karl mounted 130-foot pole with a 40-foot
sway at the top. Idle periods called for daring attempts.

While on tour with Circus Busch in Berlin, Karl was introduced to a young woman named Martha Schepp, who was a
ballerina in Circus Busch. Immediately Karl fell in love, despite the fact that his new girlfriend was deathly afraid of
heights. In addition, he knew he had committed himself to
Lena. So what was he to do about Martha? Leave Lena? If
he did that, he'd also lose her affection as well as her performance in the Wallenda wire act. His solution was obvious:
rendezvous with Martha, find excuses to leave Lena so he
could meet Martha wherever he could without being seen.
But Lena wasn't stupid. She soon figured out that her once
devoted partner now had little more than a cursory glance
for her. Lena began to simmer—at first not noticeably, but
as Karl's affair with Martha continued, her once-placid per-
sonality changed. Finally, Lena hatched an incredible
scheme that would allow her to take revenge on her unfaith-
ful lover.

One night when Karl sneaked off again to see Martha,
Lena waited up for him. As he tip-toed to his bedroom, she
waited shrouded in darkness. Suddenly, she lunged at him
screaming, flashing a single-edged razor. She went for his
face, but Karl artfully dodged her. The encounter ended
their relationship. Lena quit both Karl and the troupe. Karl
thought he had seen the last of her.

Karl immediately proposed to Martha, but her father
wouldn't let her marry, because she was too young. Karl
accepted this, thinking he could at least go on seeing her
without recourse from Lena. But then, about a month later,
as Martha and Karl neared a stage door, out jumped Lena

who had lain in wait, holding a bottle bubbling with liquid. Instantly Karl moved in front of his girlfriend, protecting Martha's face from the bottle of sulfuric acid. He grabbed the bottle from Lena, yelling at her. Without a word Lena turned from him and walked away.

In a small cafe near where Lena had attacked the duo, Karl tried to calm down a hysterical Martha, telling her that everything was all right and that Lena wouldn't bother them again. However, Martha couldn't seem to calm down, patting dry her wet eyes. Finally she blurted out while sniffling, "I lied; I'm only fifteen . . . and pregnant."

The announcement shocked Karl. Now what? Another mouth to feed. And yet, he began to plan to immediately marry Martha. They were to wed soon after in 1927, but not long after that, the marriage began to fall apart. Just as Martha had stolen Karl's love from Lena, another girl stole his love from Martha.

It began innocently. As shocking as Martha's age and pregnancy were to Karl, her phobia of heights was equally stunning. He realized she'd do him no good in his wire act. He advertised for another girl.

Sixteen-year-old Helen Kreis answered the ad. Helen went up to Karl and said she was the one for the job. Karl looked at her, studying her physique, noticing her manner, and nodded. Petite and blond, Helen also hailed from an entertainment family. Her parents' livelihood centered on amusement park rides while her choice of a career focused on circus artistry. She had spent most of her time at her uncle's circus before moving on to the highwire. Young, vivacious, and daring, Helen not only performed fearlessly on Karl's shoulders while they were on the wire, but she also demonstrated a natural poise and agility in all her performances.

* * *

Not long after Helen joined the troupe, Karl, Herman, and Helen excitedly headed to Cuba for a twelve-week engagement. First they stopped in Berlin because Martha, who was expecting her and Karl's first child, was about to give birth. The child, named Jenny, was born in a trailer on October 8, 1927, in Duisberg, Germany.

Says Jenny, "My earliest memory was when [Daddy] held me in his arms and walked the wire, telling me, 'Jenny, *Liebchen,* some day we will perform together.' My dream, cherished since childhood, was to perform on the highwire with Daddy."[4]

After Jenny's birth, the troupe continued on to Berlin where they stayed for two weeks before departing for Cuba. Martha opted to remain in Germany with her child for a while, and Herman's wife LuLu (his distant cousin) stayed there as well, to tend to their new baby, a boy who they had named Gunther.

There are many accounts of how John Ringling snatched up the Wallendas after seeing their act in Cuba. Thrilled at the prospect of steady work and a fine paying job (he was to later realize he could have and should have gotten more money out of Ringling), Karl immediately agreed to a contract when Ringling offered it to him. Karl's troupe headed for America, where they soon discovered that customs differed greatly from European ones.

Their first performance for Ringling, in March 1923 (when Karl was only twenty-three), was before 15,000 spectators in Madison Square Garden. The stunning highwire act resulted in an explosion of foot stomping, hands slamming together, and outrageous whistling. Such an outburst in Europe meant that the audience hated the act. The Wallendas figured they had flopped, so they quickly rushed back to their dressing room to hide.

Pounding on their dressing room door, Fred Bradna, the top-hatted ringmaster called, "You must come out! With all that screaming and hooting, the show can't go on until you return to the arena."

Karl grimaced. He told Bradna, "The audience hates us and are out to get us for wasting their money."

Bradna laughed. "No, no, Wallenda. Such a demonstration means the opposite in the New World—that the act is a triumph."

The amazed Wallendas returned to the ring and were greeted by a fifteen-minute round of applause. Immediately they became an international success and the pride of the Ringling Brothers.

Although the physical distance had been hard on both of them, Martha felt her love for Karl would spontaneously rekindle their affection and all would be fine again. However, when she saw her husband and Helen together, Martha instantly sensed that Helen had somehow replaced her in Karl's affection. Meanwhile Helen had constructed a myth about herself—that she was not interested in love because "love and the highwire do not go together." Martha didn't buy this, and she worried about losing Karl. Equally hard on her was learning the English language and American customs. Even more difficult was living on the road with the Ringling circus and its 1,600 employees, three full-length trains, three rings inside the big top and four stages, and sixty-four people sharing the same train car. The company was so big that wherever it set up, maps of the lay-out were provided to all employees. For shy Martha this seemed like being in the midst of a giant, frenetic ant hill, but she was determined to stay with her husband. Although Martha did not always participate in the highwire act, she did become an all-around showgirl who filled in wherever she was needed. However, she soon realized that permanently living on the road with the circus was no way to raise Jenny. Martha began considering a return to Germany—something that would turn into a routine for her: returning to Germany and then, after a short time, going back to America to be with Karl.

By 1929, the Wallendas were still employed by Ringling (they would stay with the company off and on for sixteen years, from 1928 to 1938, and then again from 1942 to 1946) and found themselves performing in St. Paul for the Osman Shrine Temple. One night, distracted by a small blast, Helen fell 40 feet off the wire, suffering significant bruising and pain. This didn't stop Karl, who was always scheming for ideas for even more daring stunts that would put his troupe on every billboard around the world. His philosophy, as he described it, was one of taking "a stunt one step beyond what is thought of as ordinary. . . . Right or wrong, this became the motivating factor of my professional life." He despaired when other acts copied his and he grew obsessed with creating an act that could not be duplicated.

Karl racked his brain for new stunts—ones that would be too difficult to copy. Later that year he had Joe Geiger and Herman ride bikes across the wire in a three-person pyramid, with Karl crouched on a chair that wobbled on a bar linking Herman and Joe. Helen had to climb atop Karl's shoulders and stand upright, facing Death straight in the eye. Without bikes, this is a very dangerous act; with bikes, it's insane. The phrase "Catch the wire if you start to fall" had been brainwashed into wire walkers' minds, but they never practiced catching the wire. With bikes, they would fall outward, away from the wire, and hence would be doomed to meet the ground.

From 1931 to 1934, Karl concentrated on assembling a second act to satisfy John Ringling's request. In this act, Martha worked the highwire with Helen's brother, Philip, doing the back-revolve. With Karl in America was his family. He put his stepfather George Grotefant in charge of the second act and called it "The Grotefants," which included Karl's brothers Willy and Arthur and Herman's wife LuLu besides Martha, Philip, and George. All seemed to be going well, but Karl had reservations about Willy, who appeared uncomfortable on the wire.

During 1931 three-year-old Jenny arrived in America intending to live with her parents Karl and Martha on Ringling Brothers' grounds. On July 26, 1931, *The Detroit Free Press* featured a picture of little Jenny, four, riding on the back of a car. She stayed with Karl and Martha for an entire season, but at the end, she returned to Germany to stay with her grandparents; then she came back to America and again stayed with her parents. During the next years Jenny went back and forth, attending school in Germany until she returned to America permanently.

Meanwhile Martha came upon her better half in bed with Helen. Upset over her husband's infidelity, she intended to return to Germany with her daughter and parents. However, Karl begged and pleaded with her to stay and said it was only one incident, an isolated mistake that wouldn't happen again. So Martha left for Germany with the understanding that she and Karl had made up.

However, while in Germany, Martha received a radio-telegram from Mexico dated November 12, 1934:

MARTHA WALLENDA BREMEN WSL.
HUSBAND FILED DIVORCE COMMUNICATE WITH ME AIRMAIL

Subsequent correspondence from the Mexican lawyer stated (in Spanish) that Karl had filed for divorce from Martha on the grounds of "incompatibility of temperaments." According to the lawyer, their marriage of 1927 in Duisberg, Germany, was dissolved, with neither having acquired community property. Karl, however, had agreed to provide for their child Jenny.

Martha wrote back to the attorney:

Dear Sir:

I am quite confused. My husband accompanied me to visit our child. He has no grounds for divorce. I am returning. Thank you.

Yours truly,
Martha Wallenda

Despite Martha's disagreement, Karl went ahead and obtained the Mexican divorce. As far as he was concerned, his and Martha's relations were severed and he was free to do as he pleased; and what he did, was to marry Helen.

Even though his personal life was tumultuous, Karl Wallenda was not distracted from his major goal, to make his act untouchable. Because of his determination, the troupe experienced a couple of close calls with bikes, one of which got them the name "The Flying Wallendas"—a name Karl disliked. But close calls or not, he brushed off the near-accidents and reassured his troupe that the Wallendas were invincible up on the wire. He did not see the close calls as omens, as death lurking in the shadows. Yet, he must have somehow sensed something, maybe even had a premonition about his brother Willy. When an accident landed Willy in the hospital for nine months, Karl tried to get Willy to consider something less perilous than the highwire, but like Karl, Willy was stubborn. He insisted on riding bikes across the wire. Nothing Karl said could dissuade him. The following season Karl received word that while Willy was performing in Sweden, a strong wind slammed into his bike and toppled him into the net. With a huge force he bounced out onto the cement floor and died instantly.

Karl was devastated by the loss of his little brother. Worse, he felt guilty for not forcing Willy to give up the highwire when he knew his brother was unsuited for such danger.

Not only had he lost Willy but, in Detroit Helen started to have fevers that rose mercilessly to 105 degrees. The diagnosis: typhoid, a deadly contagious disease. Likewise, Helen's younger sister, Yetty, came down with the same disease, as did many others in the Ringling company. Yetty had contracted such a bad case that she lost most of her hair. As if the illness of his family were not depressing enough, Karl too began showing signs of the infection. He had an unremitting low-grade temperature. All the same, he went on with work but constantly felt as though he was functioning in a dazed state. The simplest acts, ones that were once second nature to him, now became strenuous and difficult. Yet his strong constitution eventually regenerated his health. Many others succumbed to the ravages of typhoid. Helen temporarily lost her hearing from it and spent nearly two months in the hospital, chalking up a bill that would take Karl a decade to pay off.

When Helen was finally discharged, Karl decided that everyone needed to go to Florida to recuperate—a trip that marked the beginning of the Wallendas' seasonal retreat to Sarasota. Ringling personnel had been going to the spot for years. More circus people began doing the same and soon the small town became an annual off-season resort and the home of circus people worldwide. Rumors have it that Karl proposed to Helen on the highwire about this time, but in reality he married her in June while on tour with Ringling. The ceremony was held between the matinee and evening performances. The couple decided to set up home in the former sleepy village of Sarasota, where many Wallendas and other circus personnel still reside.

With a new wife to share his life, Karl felt rejuvenated and believed nothing could distract him from his dream of being the greatest highwire artist of all time.

THREE

A New Country,
A New Life

In the mid-1930s, while on sabbatical from Ringling to perform in Europe, Karl decided to bring his family and troupe back to America since it appeared war might erupt at anytime between Germany and Great Britain. However, this was no easy chore; the Wallendas had German passports. They tried unflaggingly to get back to the States. Finally they managed to get a boat back, leaving Karl's eleven-year-old daughter Jenny in Nazi Germany. Six days later war broke out. For six years, Karl received no word from or about his twelve-year-old daughter. Although Karl had a good troupe, a wonderful wife, and another child on the way, he was greatly saddened by the separation from Jenny. He, Helen, and the other troupe members left for America where his ex, Martha, planned to wed a man named Jack Mitchell.

However, Jack and Martha's marriage was not a happy one. A year after they exchanged vows, Martha divorced him. While Martha was severing ties from her second husband, Karl was mentally creating a new act—one that he would initiate when his family had their feet firmly planted on the Land of the Free and Home of the Brave. However, when he and his wife Helen and their troupe did arrive in New York City, they found themselves flat broke, prompting Karl to say, "One day you eat the chicken, the next day you eat the feathers." With the perseverance that was a hallmark, Karl worked hard to get bookings in Massachusetts with fairs, Shrine circuses, and whatever he could find to make ends meet. Eventually the Wallendas returned to Ringling.

When Russia invaded Germany, Jenny at last learned from an American soldier that her parents were alive and well. She observed, "My family was all right! I quickly wrote [to them], and we exchanged many letters this way until regular channels were reopened." With much determination on his part, Karl managed to get permission for Jenny to leave Europe for America. "When I finally arrived in the States, I kissed the soil of this beloved land," remarked Jenny.[5] For several years afterward she lived with her mother Martha.

Karl, in the meantime, continued designing ways to bring to fruition his seven-man pyramid idea. His brother Herman tried to dissuade him, saying it was too dangerous and no one in the family should risk it. Karl would not listen and kept planning his incredible stunt until it became a stunning and shocking reality.

Gunther, Herman's son, declared, "The first time the seven-man was put together, it was done on the ground. We practiced it several times a day, starting a few feet off the ground, and then working our way to moving the wire higher up until we could do it 30 feet off the ground. Of course we didn't use a net, which was our trademark, and doing the seven-man pyramid without one made us more competitive and marketable."

But Karl pressed on planning his seven-man pyramid.

* * *

The decade of the 1940s roared in like a giant wielding an axe. First, Martha decided to marry circus veterinarian J.Y. Henderson to whom Karl and Helen had introduced her. However, when Martha filed for a divorce against Jack, she learned to her amazement that she wasn't eligible. "And why not?" she asked the clerk.

"Because you're already married."

"To whom am I already married, besides Jack Mitchell?"

"Karl Wallenda."

"How? He filed papers in Mexico."

"A Mexican divorce isn't legal in the United States, and so you and Karl Wallenda are, by American law, still married. You have to get a proper American divorce from him first."

Helen was not the only one to have a large problem. Karl, who had now been married to Helen for seven years, was committing bigamy. Immediately Martha and Karl sought a legitimate divorce so that she could, in turn, divorce Jack Mitchell in order to marry J.Y. The final decree read:

IN THE CIRCUIT COURT OF THE TWELFTH
JUDICIAL CIRCUIT OF FLORIDA, IN AND FOR
SARASOTA COUNTY

Karl Wallenda, Plaintiff, vs.
Martha Wallenda also known as Martha Wallenda Mitchell, defendant

FINAL DECREE OF DIVORCE

It is, therefore, ordered, adjudged and decreed, that the bonds of matrimony . . . are hereby dissolved.

It is further ordered, adjudged and decreed that the

parties jointly shall have the care, control and supervision of their minor child, Jennie [*sic*] Ella Wallenda, now 12 years of age; that for the present said minor child shall remain in the custody of her maternal grandmother, Mrs. Ella Schepp who resides in the city of Berlin, Germany; that in the event said child shall come or be brought to the United States . . . then each of the parties shall have the custody of her for six months out of each year and that at all times both parties shall have an equal voice concerning her education and rearing;

It is further ordered, adjudged and decreed, that the plaintiff pay to the said Mrs. Ella Schepp the sum of $25.00 monthly for the care, maintenance and support of said minor child. . . .

Done and ordered at Fort Myers, Florida, this 20th day of March, A.D. 1940. [signed by the circuit judge]

Two years later, one of the worst devastations to hit showfolk occurred in Cleveland. Helen stood scrubbing laundry on the Cleveland Ringling grounds with her daughter Carla, who was seven, at her side. The child was entertaining herself by watching the hustle and bustle of circus life around her. Then something caught the little girl's attention. She yelled out, "Look Mommy! The tent with the animals is on fire!"

Because of the war, paraffin canvas was the only type of tent available. The inferno raged, eating up the paraffin canvases. Thirty-six animals died in the fire: elephants, camels, zebras, lions, tigers, giraffes, gnus.

A few years later, while the world was still immersed in war, another circus fire broke out. Ringling had been debating the logic of touring since manpower and materials, including the much-needed flame-proof canvas, were at a premium. People seemed to need the joy of the circus and on July 6, in Hartford, Connecticut, the large number of people under the big top made showfolk and circus owners dance with glee. For them, this was one of the happiest moment in their lives—bleachers filled with the smiling faces of parents who took their children to see the circus. Performers hurried and scurried about in anticipation of playing to a full house, and owners counted the money as lines of spectators entered the tent.

Karl climbed the platform at one end of the wire, followed by Herman, Yetty (Helen's sister), and Joe Geiger. At the other end of the wire stood Helen on the platform, waiting for the troupe to assemble at the opposite end in order to begin the act. The house buzzed as it filled with eager spectators, over seven thousand people, most of whom were mothers with their children. Helen watched as Herman climbed the platform to join his brother Karl. Then she looked at her husband for a signal to begin; Karl nodded. Suddenly, directly behind him she caught a flash, as though a huge lightning bug went flickering past. Then came the sparking. She yelled to Karl, "Look behind you!"

By her urgency and expression, he knew something was wrong. He spun around, feeling a surge of torches above his head. The second he looked up, he saw the fire consuming the paraffin canvas. With the crackling came flames speeding like wildfire across the tent top, down its sides, maniacally eating the wax, burgeoning with greater force, gulping oxygen, growing, racing chaotically throughout the tent. Karl screamed to his troupe to get down off the wire, and as they slid down the ropes, the band played the traditional music, "Stars and Stripes Forever," that warned of trouble.

The Wallendas bounded to the ground and instantly got caught up in the hysterical crowds stampeding to the exit, thus scattering the troupe among the visitors. Everyone shoved, pushed, screeched, and shrieked as they scrambled around the big top trying to make it outside. Joe and Karl got out, but Helen, who managed to get off the platform and on the ground, became enmeshed in the berserk mob. She found herself pinned against the steel rigging. She was afraid she would be trampled to death by the crazed hordes who were pushing and tromping on fallen children and women or being burned by plummeting chunks of fiery paraffin and sheets of collapsing, flaming canvas. Helen remained wedged between the animal chutes and the steel rigging. She felt the ground vibrate with running feet and heard mothers frantically scream for children who had been squashed or bulldozed over.

In the meantime, Herman and his son Gunther were also frantically searching for a way out. Gunther describes the scene this way: "The show with the animals was closing and they were taking down the chutes, so we had just gotten on the wire. I remember I became aware of people quickly moving from their seats, and when I looked around, I saw the fire which had started at the entrance. It hit the preheated big top, catching the canvas ceiling on fire. When you're up that high on the wire, you can feel the heat near the ceiling. When it hit the canvas ceiling, it was instantaneous; the whole thing only took five minutes.

"At first everything was orderly and calm, and then everyone went crazy. I saw a guy swinging a chair around. The panic was the worst; people didn't think to use the side entrance. There were kids trying to get back into the fiery tent to retrieve their peanuts. It was just crazy. My father and I managed to save ourselves by going out the performers' entrance near the animal chutes. No entertainers died in that fire, but there were a lot of parents and kids who did—many just got trampled to death."

Most of the deaths were attributed to suffocation from the fallen smoldering canvas; some were due to people blindly running into steel. Many spectators were smashed to death; while still others caught on fire and burned. Three-foot piles of charred, foul-smelling bodies spotted the big top.

Helen, who remained wedged in the rigging, watching the piles grow, became more and more terrified. The uncontrolled fires flamed hot enough to pucker and buckle paint on vehicles parked outside the tent. The band played on until the main supporting poles gave way; then the musicians ran for their lives. Helen was sure she was damned. She lay entangled, waiting for her death.

Suddenly, out of nowhere, her brother Philip appeared. He had been up in the bleachers when the first spark flashed. Now he looked downward and saw Helen lying on the ground. With shear determination, he broke through the hysterical multitude and pulled his older sister out of her death trap to safety.

When it was all over, 170 people had perished from asphyxiation, nearly 500 more suffered burns and other injuries. Six hundred claims were filed for a whopping four million dollars, enough to do any circus company in. However, Ringling vowed to make it right. He spent nine years paying off the debt from receipts of later performances. The Hartford fire went down in the records as *the* most atrocious accident in the history of circus tradition. For circus people who still speak of it with great sorrow, it remains a reminder of what they have forever lost.

Still the circus tradition went on, and Karl continued to plan the seven-man human pyramid which had been Karl's dream since 1938. Finally, in the late 1940s, it neared reality, it was possible; practice had proved it. Practice had shown that the wire could hold the weight of seven performers, with their poles, a chair, and all those extra guy wires. They had put a girl at the top (top-mounter) of the pyramid because she weighed less than a man, so now, everything seemed ready, but against the better judgment of Herman, who protested, "Karl, this is a damned dangerous trick. One person slips—the whole lot goes. Not many outside of our family will risk it."[6]

Despite these hazards, Karl was determined to perform what would be the most sensational act ever, and one not likely to be duplicated by anyone. Surely he would go down in history for such an electrifying stunt. All he had to do was convince family members that it could be done, and done safely. He became driven, and he drove his family with the same passion.

Night and day they attempted the human pyramid, over and over again, always with Karl calling out orders, herding, coercing, forcing the troupe to practice, practice, practice. Exhausted, everyone would drop in their beds late at night, their arms aching from holding the pole, their minds throbbing from the tension. Just one little slip by any one of them would result in the act's disintegration, and, most likely, the resultant death of everyone. Karl pressed harder to achieve his dream.

For Karl, 1947 finally brought the fulfillment of another desire. His daughter Jenny, who was twenty that year, joined his wire act. Immediately she became engulfed in her father's goal to make the seven-man pyramid the greatest act on earth.

And then, like a bolt of lightning streaking through a clear sky, it happened. Suddenly everything meshed—body movements in complete harmony, steps in exact alignment, breathing as though the seven were a hydra, a collective animal, moving slowly, snail-like along the wire in perfect consonance. The troupe had perfected it so well, they managed to top themselves by building an eight-man pyramid, but the performers decided against it—too much weight; seven men proved to be ideal. Karl's fantasy turned into rhapsody. At last he had accomplished his goal. And he was right—no one could top this act. Everyone talked about it around the world; jobs were no longer scarce for the Wallendas. At each performance of the pyramid, astonished audiences oohed and aahed, some closing their eyes lest the worst occur, others holding their breaths as Karl and the others moved along the wire with only the sound of slippers sliding against the wire. When they finally stepped onto the opposite platform, there would come a loud unified sigh and then deafening hoots and whelps as bystanders jumped to their feet, applauding.

Always the seven-man played before packed houses. And the Wallendas would stand on the platform, grinning widely, waving their arms, the spectators waving back, blowing kisses, generating a love-affair between them and the Great Wirewalkers. What more could Karl ask for in life? This . . . this sound of love . . . the bravado—was it not what life was all about?

From 1947 to 1962, the Wallendas performed "the seven" without anything going wrong, and no other troupe could copy them. By then, sixteen years had passed without the slightest problem. They were the masters. During this period, besides accomplishing the seven-man pyramid, the Wallendas had mastered other feats, building a repertoire of such acts as "Les Sylphides"[7]—women hanging by their teeth—wondrous acrobatics, and, of course, the high pole where Yetty climbed the 140-foot flexible pole and swayed back and forth on it. Not only did it take her time to climb the lofty staff, but it required long minutes for her to de-

scend—too much wasted time in a show. So Karl incorporated the slide-for-life technique into her act: Yetty looped
her foot to a long wire—somewhere around 200–350 feet—
and slid down the side of the cable. It was ingenious; not
only did it save precious minutes but it was thrilling and
daring.

About this time, adding to Karl's happiness, Jenny prepared to marry a dashing young man—Alberto Zoppe. The
Zoppe family hailed from Italy and were great bareback riders, having founded their own circus back in the mid-1800s.
Alberto followed the tradition, remaining in the business
and going on to become one of the top riders in Circo Italia
and also in the Circus Europa. For Jenny, Alberto seemed to
be perfect. A short time after her wedding, Jenny became
pregnant with their first child. The Wallenda family seemed
filled with good fortune. A few months later, however, the
first dark shadow fell across their paths.

Jenny and Alberto were riding on a Ringling train when
her water broke. Jenny had no idea of what was happening.
When the train stopped, her new sister-in-law told her she
was having the baby. Alberto took her to the nearest hospital. Unfortunately, the doctor administered so much ether to
her that it killed the baby. They named him Alan. He was
born and buried in San Antonio. It was the first, but not the
last, touch of darkness.

Not long afterward, the Circus Wallenda demonstrated
that even the best can fail when attendance declines over a
period of time—something attributable to a loss of affection
for the art by once enamored audiences. But Karl plodded
on and prodded others along with him. At any cost, he
would proceed with the seven-man pyramid. He needed the
rush, the applause; and besides, he wanted to continue to
show the world that the Wallendas had cornered the market
on dauntlessness.

* * *

And then in 1950, needing employment, the Wallendas went to work for the Clyde Beatty Circus. One day they had to drive from Philadelphia to Nebraska for an engagement. Helen took the wheel in order to give Karl a rest from the long, monotonous drive. A bit disconnected by the unfamiliar road, she accelerated so that she might keep up with Philip, who was driving the rigging truck not too far ahead. Suddenly, a huge black bird slammed into Helen's windshield. Helen's mother screamed, "That means death in the family!"[8]

Wanting to calm her, Helen replied, "No, it means nothing; that's just German folklore." She continued to drive on but lost sight of Philip's vehicle.

When Helen and her passengers finally arrived in Nebraska, Philip was still nowhere to be found. Helen's mother became hysterical. At first Karl and Helen tried reassuring her that all was fine; yet they themselves wondered where Philip possibly could have gone. Everyone thought that perhaps he had stopped for a bite to eat. However, Helen was worried though she tried not to show it. Philip was special to her; she owed him her life, and she liked his braveness and excitement about American life. He had adapted quickly to the new country, even marrying an American girl. They had exchanged vows on the highwire. The marriage, however, was short-lived. His wife had died in childbirth, leaving behind their three-day-old son Mario for Philip to raise. "What kind of life will Mario have?" Philip had said to his sister and Karl a few days after his wife died. "He needs a mother, too, not a father who lives like a gypsy." Helen and Karl offered to raise him, and Philip agreed.

Feeling more apprehensive now, Helen saw no signs of

Philip's whereabouts. Her worrying intensified; her brother should have arrived long ago. More time passed and still Philip didn't appear.

Then a telegram came. While Philip had been changing a flat alongside the road, a drunk driver had swerved and bulldozed him. Philip was dead.

Soon after, Mario Kreis was officially adopted by Karl and Helen, making him Mario Wallenda.

The rest of that year seemed to spiral downhill. Philip's death appeared to be a bad omen.

And then, one of those small miracles occurred which seem to revitalize ones faith in life.

Jenny, Karl's beloved daughter, became pregnant again. In September she had a son, Tino. Two years later, when the Wallendas' fortune seemed on the rise again, she gave birth to a daughter, Delilah, whom Jenny named after the character Delilah in Cecil B. deMille's *The Greatest Show on Earth*.

FOUR

Destined for the Highwire

Dear Mr. and Mrs. Zoppe:

Mr. deMille asked me to thank you for the announcement [of Delilah's birth], and to congratulate you on the arrival of [her birth]. If she's anything like little Albertino [Tino, Delilah's older brother], you'll have the two most beautiful children in the world. And the next time I see Heddy Lamarr, I'll tell her she can look for stiff competition from the newest Delilah.

We heard you are no longer with the Ringling show this year. But I'm sure you had a very successful season.

At present, we are working on the next film which is to be THE TEN COMMANDMENTS.

I still have two photographs and I shall send you as soon as I get them autographed by Chuck Heston and Gloria Grahame.

All your friends here join me in wishing you (and cucci-olo) a very Happy New Year.

Sincerely,

Bernice Mosk
Office of C. D. DeMille
[dated December 30, 1952]

Delilah Zaira Diana Zoppe's arrival in Sarasota—the circus capital of the world—on Friday, December 18, 1952, created new joy in the Wallenda family. Everyone fussed over and bustled about her, especially Mutti Martha, Karl's first wife and Jenny's mother.[9] Even step-grandmother Mutti Helen nuzzled and cuddled the Christmas baby, who was baptized:

CERTIFICATE OF BAPTISM
St. Martha's Church

This is to certify that *Delilah Zaira Diana Zoppe* child of *Giovanni Alberto Zoppe* and *Jenny Ella Wallenda* born in *Sarasota, Fla.* on the *18th* day of *Dec. 1952* was baptized on the *24th* day of *Dec. 1952* according to the rite of the Roman Catholic Church by the Rev. *Robert A. Hastler* the sponsors being *Juan Rodriguez* and *Helen Wallenda* as appears from the Baptismal Register of this church. Dated *Dec. 24, 1952*. [signed by the priest and Helen Wallenda]

Delilah certainly benefited from an extended family and an older brother who seemed protective of her. At three months old, she accompanied her parents, who were performing in Rochester. While there, Jenny noticed the cold the child had was worsening. She rushed Delilah to the doctor.

The physician, tugging the stethoscope off his ears, announced, "She has pneumonia, and if you continue to take her on the road, she'll die."

Despairing, Jenny and Alberto discussed what to do. They had to work, and none of the family members were around to help care for the baby. Then they heard about a couple who took children in. The Zoppes talked some more and checked out the couple. They finally decided, with great reluctance, that they must think of the best interest of their child, and they left Delilah with William and Clara, who had an adopted daughter.

Throughout the months Jenny was away, she greatly missed her baby. She couldn't wait for the tour to end. When the moment finally arrived six months later, she hurried to William and Clara's house to get Delilah, who was then nine months old. "I can't wait to see her," said Jenny, as she nervously peered into the other room, hoping to catch sight of her baby daughter.

William and Clara shook their heads. "Well, you'll have to wait; you can't have Delilah. We've taken care of her for months now, and we think she'll be better off with us."

"You mean for good?" asked Jenny, shocked.

"We're too attached to her. We're going to keep her, love her, give her a stable home—not one where the parents are here one day and not the next. Besides," claimed Clara, "you haven't even paid us for babysitting, like we agreed. No money, no kid."

"I want my child! Now!" Jenny screamed.

"First you better get us our money," Clara and William retorted, "then we'll see. The child would be better off with us."

And of course, Jenny won. The couple had to back down.

They knew their argument would not stand up in court, even if it got that far. Jenny was ecstatic. For months she had been envisioning this event, waiting for her offspring to come squealing and yelping, jumping into her arms. How many times she had imagined them hugging and snuggling, touching warm cheek to warm cheek, and Jenny would nuzzle her baby all over, whispering hundreds of "I love yous." Bill and Clara left the room. Eagerly Jenny waited but heard nothing. Jenny shifted from side to side, looking around the room, cocking her ear to hear her baby call out, "Mama, Mama." The house remained silent. "Delilah, Delilah, Delilah," she called. Still no baby.

Finally Clara appeared with the child. Jenny stretched out her arms. The smile on her face grew wider as she smelled Delilah's sweet, powdery baby smell. She moved forward to scoop Delilah into her bosom. But the child shook her head back and forth, her face puckering as she eyed the strange woman before her.

"Come on, honey. Come to Mama." Jenny reached over to take Delilah from Clara.

The baby drew back and tossed her head back and forth, more determined than ever to stay with the woman who has taken care of her. *Why is she doing this, wanting to take me away from the arms of the only woman I know as Mother?*

"Delilah, come on now," Jenny pleaded.

The child spun away from Jenny and squashed her body hard against Clara. Noooooo, she would never go with that stranger! her little nails dug deep into Clara's back as she cried out with fear. Finally Jenny pried her away, clutching Delilah and vowing never to let her child get away again.

* * *

A year later, while America was engulfed in the Korean war, Jenny Wallenda and Alberto Zoppe were engulfed in a war of their own. On the outside, everything seemed wonderful—Jenny and Alberto the parents of two beautiful children—while on the inside, the couple was quarrelsome and unhappy. They decided to separate, hoping that distance would rekindle their old love. And while Jenny agonized over her deteriorating marriage, she was also worrying about what to do with her children since she would have to return to work to support them. Moreover, she worried about finding a job. The answer to that dilemma came when her father invited her to perform in Colombia, South America, with his troupe. Quickly, Jenny accepted.

Then she realized she desperately needed someone to care for her children. The frightening situation with Clara and William had convinced her she couldn't trust strangers. Jenny opted to leave the children with her mother Martha while she performed.

Before she left the country, Jenny made one last attempt to reconcile with Alberto. They did talk things out, with Alberto claiming he wanted their marriage to work. Jenny decided to go back to Alberto, but then she discovered that he had a woman living with him. It was over. Thereafter, Delilah's grandfather Karl (Vati), step-grandfather J.Y., brother Tino, and the circus became the center of Delilah's small universe.

> "Performers' children grow up a lot faster than children who live permanently at home. . . . They acquire common sense sooner, and they're exposed to a lot more," says Delilah Wallenda, who remembers being spanked as a toddler whenever she lost her balance on the low wire and didn't try to catch it. "I was destined for this— the high wire, the skywalks."

* * *

The closeness of the Wallendas came from one common interest—the wire. Everyone Delilah knew, even as a small child, lived and breathed performing. Though most of the Wallendas—including aunts, uncles, cousins, grandparents —spent their lives on the road, some together and others apart doing separate bookings, the family still managed to remain emotionally connected. Delilah was especially close to Vati, who played with her all the time, inculcating his love of the highwire. "I always had a good time with him. I remember as a child, he would play with us and do tricks with us. I would stand in his hands as he held me, or he would put me on his shoulders and I wuld stand erect with my hands out, like a wirewalker balancing herself. We'd just do things together, laughing all the time. He could persuade me to try tricks—stunts that for a non-circus kid would be dangerous and frightening—and I would do them without fear because he was so reassuring. And the way he smiled, how his eyes looked, I had total trust in him. I believe he could convince anyone to do anything, he was such a charmer!"

Karl was her idol. Delilah's other major influence was her grandmother, Martha. Nearly every day they spent time talking, going places, reading the Bible. J.Y., Martha's husband, was kind, too, but it was Martha whom Delilah was close to and with whom she often stayed when her mother was away.

While Delilah was there one day, a loud knock resounded from the front door. Martha opened it. "Hello, Alberto," she said.

"I've come to take my children back home with me," a dark-haired, good-looking man with a deep voice stated.

Mutti stared at him, then nodded and opened the door for him.

Delilah watched the man enter the house. She sensed that she knew him, had seen him before. Suddenly she realized it was her father. Should she run to him and hug him? Or run behind Mutti's waist and hide in the folds of her dress?

"Come on, kids. Get your stuff together," he told them.

Packed and having said goodbyes, Delilah and Tino headed for their father's car. Little Delilah looked back longingly at Mutti. She wanted to run into her grandmother's arms, to be held, protected, anchored, but her father was ushering her into the back seat of the car. She sat rigidly and waited for the engine to start, tears running down her cheeks.

Again, she had been shifted from family to family, her life torn apart. She whimpered all the way to Alberto's house, fearing she would never see her mother again. She believed Mutti had betrayed her by giving her up to another stranger.

Living with her father confused Delilah even more, because she couldn't figure out why he had taken her and how the people around him fit into her life. She ended up calling her father's sister "Mommy."

Meanwhile, Jenny was away on a tour of South America. She had no idea that her children now lived with her ex-husband, Alberto.

While on tour her friendship with her old friend Dick Faughnan had become a romance. Though he was four years younger than she, Dick seemed mature and committed to her.

Jenny first met Dick when he had worked on the Ringling show in the animal department; then, when he moved on to work for Karl, they became better friends. Dick had asked Karl for a job. But Karl said, "You have to have your parents' permission in writing, and if then you're still interested, visit Sarasota where the circus's winter quarters are."

Dick did just that, and Karl kept his promise, giving the young Faughnan a job setting up equipment. Dick had worked his way up and was now performing on the highwire in Columbia, South America with Jenny.

Dick finally proposed to her, she accepted, and they married in South America.

Upon returning home, with Dick at her side, Jenny went directly to her mother's house. She looked around but didn't see her children. "Where are Tino and Delilah?" she asked, suddenly frightened.

Martha answered, "Alberto came for them. I let them go because I thought you and he had arranged it."

"He *stole* my children!" screamed Jenny. She stormed over to Alberto's and told him, "I'll get them back no matter what I have to do." She immediately got an emergency court order that Tino and Delilah not be allowed to leave the country, because she was afraid Alberto would take them to Italy and she would never see them again. Then she got a court order to have her children returned.

With the children back in her home, Jenny and Dick embarked on a new life, but for Delilah it was a familiar style, one that was on the road, off the road, tottering like a see-saw on a playground. Soon little Delilah came to realize that her mother's leaving her with others while she worked in the circus was to be a regular and frustrating cycle.

Adjusting once again to a new family was neither easy nor quick for Delilah. Much of her early formative years had already been determined by others. Adapting was even more trying because there was a new person in her mother's life—someone named Dick. Delilah didn't know who he was; she only knew that he was vying for her mother's attention.

From then on, while Jenny and Dick were off performing

in the seven-man pyramid, Delilah would visit in other people's homes. Every year from November to February,
Martha babysat Delilah while Jenny went on the road. In
other periods through the year, other relatives babysat her
as well. And although Delilah managed finally to piece together the puzzle—who Jenny was, how Dick fit into her life,
and that she did have a real father named Alberto—Delilah's
perceptions of who she was were hazy and confused. Moreover, she wasn't sure on whom she could rely for stability.

For Jenny, as for her daughter, the separations were also
difficult. Jenny too sought stability. The year 1956 saw
Jenny's signing up for various circus engagements that allowed her to remain at home with her children. However,
the day arrived when there was no work nearby and she had
to go far away. While she was gone, Alberto again came to
take Tino and Delilah away. This time he drove them to another state. When she returned, Jenny once again called the
police, but they told her they couldn't do anything because
the abduction was out of their jurisdiction. However, Alberto finally decided to return when his lawyer told him he
might be arrested for kidnapping.

At the bus station, Jenny waited for her son and daughter.
As they got off the bus Delilah was hysterical and Tino
screamed, "How can you take us away from our father!"
Despairing, Jenny turned around and took them back to Alberto.

That following November, though, the children decided to
come back to her. Jenny told them if they wanted to stay she
would no longer permit them to be with her ex-husband for
any extended period of time. Their permanent residence
would be with her. For Delilah, this proved to be one more

adjustment in a long line of changes, but once she got used to staying with her mother, and Mutti Martha when Jenny went away, Delilah began to have a sense of belonging. The four of them—herself, her mother, her brother, and Dick— became a real family. Soon Dick treated her as though she were his real daughter; even his rare punishments rein- forced their togetherness. Once, when Jenny was serving split-pea soup and Delilah refused to eat, Dick winked at Jenny and said, "Put it in a cup for Delilah." Jenny did and Delilah thought it was the best thing her mother had ever made.

As she became closer to her mother, Delilah developed an emotional bond, as well as a physical attachment, to all the Wallendas. The Wallenda tribe lived within walking and short driving distances of Delilah's home. In fact, Karl and Helen lived catty-corner from Martha and J.Y. The four vis- ited each other back and forth. As the years passed, Helen and Martha had become good friends. Martha stayed with Helen a few times when J.Y. left to work on Ringling where she later joined him. This extended nuclear clan elated not only Delilah, but Vati as well, who wanted all of his loved ones to be one big happy family.

So determined was Karl about maintaining family ties that he went to great lengths to ensure that holidays were always spent together.

"Christmas," Delilah recalls, "was his favorite time be- cause he demanded that everyone got together, traveling to one another's houses, first to his place and then, like a band, on to my grandmother's since she lived catty-corner from Karl and Helen. And all that food! Vati made sure that every- one ate, and ate, and ate. We'd go to bed Christmas night so full, we couldn't even turn on our sides. Grandfather was a wonderful man with a big heart." Smiling, Delilah adds, "When you met him, you liked him right away. He got people to do what he wanted; how, I'm not sure, but I've often thought about it. I think he just had a natural gift, a charisma about him."

To Karl, family was the most important thing in life. And obedient children that they were, neither Jenny nor sister Carla refused their father anything. The family particularly enjoyed being around him when they were out in public and the child inside him took over. Then, he reverted to playing childhood pranks on anyone near him. Delilah observes, "Sometimes something would get into him, like he had been overcome with a strange disorder, and he'd revert to playing practical jokes. In restaurants, he'd sneeze so loudly as a waitress bustled past carrying a tray of water glasses, she'd jump in surprise and drop the tray; other times he'd smash pastry into his brother's face. And still other times he'd do something as inane as chewing up pieces of paper in his mouth until they formed a soft wad, and then he'd stick it on his nose, looking around the restaurant, smiling naturally at anyone who was pointing at him. When Vati got this way, he infected everyone, and soon the whole Wallenda troupe would be acting as silly as he. You had to keep your distance from him during those times, but no matter how innocent or stand-offish you got, he'd zero right in on you and pull you into the joke. It was better to play along with him, reassuring yourself that this too would pass."

However, Karl's jocular spirit changed where his art was concerned. He was like a different man then, deadly serious about the highwire. He drove everyone to perfection, until each muscle and bone in their bodies ached. Their nerves and tendons were still jumping when he finally let them quit for the day to fall exhausted into sleep.

To his family, however, his negatives were balanced out by his positives: the family remained with him whether he was being funny, ornery, or barking orders. Each member supported the others. Even the children were close to each other. Jenny's half-sister Carla allowed her son Ricky to walk to his aunt's early each morning. There he would sit on Jenny's stoop, waiting to be let into the house to have breakfast and play with Tino and Delilah. Adds Delilah, "Through the years, we grew very close, especially my mother and Aunt Carla and, of course, her children. My mother and Aunt Carla treated each other as though they were fullblooded sisters, and my mother thought of Helen as her own mother. For Tino and me, Helen was and is like a grandmother to me. Ricky and Rietta and Tino and I always played together and fought just like brothers and sisters. Those were great years."

Delilah, who had once felt so alone, now felt as though her nuclear family reached out to include great-uncle Herman (Karl's brother), Herman's wife, Aunt Edith, and their son Gunther, as well as Mario (the adopted brother) and his wife —whom Delilah called aunt and uncle, too. All were one big family who loved and cared for each other but were closed to outsiders. They were taught and trained by Vati, the wire serving as their umbilical cord.

And then there was Marga, whose presence in the family Delilah concedes is difficult to explain. She offers, "She was my grandfather's mistress; it's the only way I can put it. We don't talk much about it, so what I know is limited, except that Vati and Marga fell in love when Helen went off to marry someone else. However, Helen changed her mind and returned to Vati, but he felt obligated to take care of Marga for the rest of her life. Mutti Helen accepted the situation, and Marga came to the family as a full-fledged member, as did Marga's niece, Patsy. I guess," Delilah observes, "in a lot of ways, we're a very complicated family."

Complicated is an understatement. The Wallendas' embrangled history is pocked with an olio of love, jealousy, greed, and yet, loyalty. Jenny, Delilah's mother adds, "Marga was never a bother to anyone. In fact, she often did nice things for the family, although not all of the Wallendas were as nice to her."

Marga's door was always open to the clan. Early in her Wallenda existence, she took Ricky in when his grandmother, Helen, became frustrated watching him in her daughter Carla's absence. Linda, the wife of Karl's son Mario, explains, "Mario and I used to take Ricky in, too, when he was younger because his mother sometimes found his high-spirited behavior difficult. We had cared for him as if he were our own son. Once he disobeyed me for the umpteenth time, so I threw him out, told him to go home or stay with Marga, whatever. And so he went to Marga's and she kept him, watched over him."

Delilah claims 1957 was one of the happiest periods in her life. It was, for the once lonely child, a wondrous time when she felt close to her family and to her cousin Ricky, who also seemed destined to follow in their ancestors' footsteps.

Delilah was five. She was discovering an exciting world, relishing the moments when the adults disappeared into "Big People Land," and left her, her brother, and cousin Ricky alone. Magically the three came together on the low-wire, first trying to balance themselves and falling, laughing the whole time, challenging each other to perform different tricks the way their parents did. Then Ricky climbed atop Tino, who called out, "C'mon, Delilah, get up on my shoulders." Trusting him, she skipped over to where he stood on the wire. He reached down and lifted her up by her arms and set her on his wide shoulders, forming their first three-person act on the wire. Sitting at the tip-top, she sensed a thrill course through her. Suddenly the three-high dissembled and she was back on the ground, staring at the fellows whose faces broke into wide smiles. They congratulated each other and talked about how they would someday become famous wirewalkers, just like their parents and grandparents, aunts and uncles. There were many wonderful nights to visit and grow in the Wallenda tradition.

However, sometimes the children's high spirits would overflow. One day when Jenny was off occupying herself with some business matter, someone approached her and asked, "Do you know where your children are?"

Jenny shrugged, confused. Of course she knew. "They're right here, playing." But when she looked around, both Tino and Delilah were not to be seen.

The friend shook her head and said, "They're playing follow-the-leader high up on the steel girders."

Jenny jumped up, ran after them, and got them down.

Still another time, while the Wallendas were performing in Cuba—at the same time Castro's coup overtook the government—Delilah and Tino were being looked after by Martha's sister Ria and Alberto's cousin Ginsana. The two kids went off to the playground. Delilah liked to frolic on the slides, see-saws, and swings, but her favorite activity was to hang on the bars to see who could jump off the farthest.

"I went farther than you," Tino teased her after he landed far out from the bars.

"But you're taller," she countered.

"Here, let me help you." He got behind her and gave her a push.

The extra boost sent the petite child flying and she landed hard on her arm. The impact stung so hard that she burst into sobs.

"Don't cry; it doesn't hurt," Tino tried soothing her.

But it did hurt, so much so that Delilah ended up in the emergency room. Hours later she left with her fractured arm in a sling. "You must rest," the doctors cautioned.

Delilah, however, was already on her way to becoming a performer though not as yet on the highwire. Imbued with "the show must go on" philosophy, not long afterward Jenny dressed her little girl in a costume and Delilah bounced out in front of an audience to hold the "come down" rope for the performers after their act so they could descend the wire. Delilah had already begun roaming the circus grounds, wearing costumes, soaking up performances, and watching all the preparation going into those exciting acts; she sat captivated as entertainers applied makeup, created costumes, designed acts. She talked to animal trainers and watched them perform with different beasts; she slept in campers while her family toured the world. Already she felt as much at home on the road as a bird did in its nest.

She was learning the Wallenda heritage. No matter what the stunt, the Wallendas stayed together, traveling in big semis carrying equipment and costumes from spot to spot, and performing. Of course, though it was an exciting life, this constant traveling put some hardships on the young Delilah, one of which was school. Delilah wanted to go on the road with her mother, but Jenny prohibited it, telling Delilah and her other children that an education was more important. She reminded them that she herself was a graduate of a business college.

For Jenny, even riding in bumpy trucks was not a good enough excuse to get out of doing homework. Jenny expected Delilah to do her schoolwork no matter what the circumstances, whether staying in a relative's cushy home or riding in a jarring circus truck. Delilah obeyed her, but her thoughts were already on the circus. On each trip, she couldn't wait for the moment when the Wallendas' wagons would come to a halt at some circus and everyone would scramble out and begin surveying the area to set up. She loved the hubbub. Then, after setting up the equipment, she got to sit under the big top and watch the performers as she added or subtracted some problems in her text. The dismantling after the show was over was almost as much fun as setting up, because Vati gave her and the other kids a dollar each to go around pulling out stakes. All the grandchildren giggled as they ran off to find the stakes and yank them out. Afterwards they ran up to Vati holding their treasure and got their dollar bills, which he always handed out with a smile, giving Delilah a special hug. But no matter how much fun Delilah was having, she was still made to obey her mother's rule that she go to school.

Attending classes on and off was difficult. Trying to catch up on what she missed was a sure disadvantage, and all too many times she had a lot of work to make up. Social relationships were also difficult to forge at school, though she had many circus friends. Not being there to build a solid long-term relationship meant she was omitted from cliques, left out of parties and other activities, and denied the opportunity to form friendships with other classmates. Not only did she have social problems, but Delilah felt that even her teachers didn't like her or that they resented her lifestyle.

One time at recess, Delilah, like all the other children in her class, was allowed to go out into the hall to use the bathroom and get a drink at the water fountain, provided they did not talk. It was the high moment of the day for the youngsters. The class left the room in an orderly fashion. All was going well. Then as Delilah stood in the line for a drink, a little girl standing in line tapped Delilah on the shoulder and asked her something. Not wanting to hurt the girl's feelings by ignoring her, Delilah tried whispering that she couldn't talk at the moment but would answer later. However, the second Delilah turned to face the girl, the teacher bounded down the hall, grabbing Delilah by her arm and dragging her back into the classroom. She pushed the frightened child back in her seat. Standing over the humiliated and wretched child, the teacher crossed her arms at her chest, stamped her feet, her eyes flitting from the children filing into the classroom back to Delilah. She waited for the entire class to return from the hall and get seated.

Then she said, "See, class, this is what happens when you don't follow the rules and the same thing will happen to you if you talk while in line." She began to paddle Delilah in front of everyone.

The normally obedient child was devastated by the humiliation. She never recovered from this indignity; from then on, Delilah clammed up and withdrew. She was turned off from learning. School grew increasingly hard for her.

Still, she was made to attend.

Seeing her depressed, Jenny and Dick worried about her almost all the time. Finally, Dick told Jenny, "I don't really want to go back on the road. You know me, I'd rather be home anyway."

Jenny nodded. "Fine, I'll go to work for my father and you stay home with the kids while they're in school."

He did, inheriting not only Delilah and Tino, but Ricky and his siblings as well. Even so, Dick was happy. And so was Delilah, who finally had a substitute father at home all the time.

FIVE

Dark Shadows

In 1959 an accident befell Margarita—the second wife of Gunther, Herman's son.

After his first marriage ended in divorce, Gunther had roamed free and unattached. While playing the Royal Dunbar Circus in Mexico City with his father and Uncle Karl, he met Margarita, whose olive-skinned, dark-haired beauty complimented his own fairness and light hair. As in prince and princess romances, they instantly fell in love and wed in Mexico.

They were soon blessed with a little girl, whom they named Sandy. Gunther had a delightful baby and a beautiful wife who also was a circus performer: a perfect marriage. He was finally happy, but then in December, right around Delilah's birthday, came a night that would forever haunt the Wallendas.

As an aerialist in the "Carousel" act, Margarita, along with other female performers, hung from a specially designed apparatus that had different sections, each formed in a perch or "lira" they did tricks on. For the finish, these lira flew up into the air, requiring the women to hook a loop onto the swivel apparatus. They put their heads through the loop so they could hang by their necks and spin while performing nimble ballet maneuvers.

On that night, as they were preparing to go on, Margarita noticed a problem in the apparatus of the girl next to her. She cautioned her, "You're not properly fastened; be sure to connect everything tightly so that nothing happens to you."

The girl smiled and said she'd do it, then she ran off towards the stage entrance. Still thinking about the young performer, Margarita finished donning her costume and then she too headed for the stage. Within minutes her act was introduced, and she and the other women ran to the lira where Margarita hung gracefully in the air in front of a packed house.

Gunther began the act by turning the rope that suspended his wife. Engrossed in carefully winding the rope, he didn't look up to see that Margarita's line was tangled and twisted at the top.

"Oh my God!" he yelled when he realized what had happened. Quickly he pulled her up. Margarita's body was limp. He rushed her to the hospital.

"Her back is fractured," the doctor said. "She shouldn't have been moved at all."

Gunther collapsed in a chair, understanding what lay ahead.

Nearly every day for eight or nine months, he visited his love in the hospital, and with each passing day came the realization that Margarita would probably never again be able to walk, certainly not without a brace.

"I have to walk normally," she protested, knowing this was also the ruination of her career.

Helplessly, Gunther replied, "You've got to work hard at getting better. Sandy and I are waiting for you to come home."

However, Margarita did not get better. She began to run fevers, and soon a kidney infection was diagnosed. "This setback," the physician told Gunther, "will require more extensive hospitalization. But she can't stay in a general hospital like this; I'm having her transferred to a rehab center where she'll get over the infection and then learn how to take care of herself again."

They transferred Margarita, but by then she had realized just how hopeless her condition was. Her spirit was broken. Not only would she be in the hospital a long time, but she would never have the full use of her legs and spine. Her condition deteriorated rapidly.

Says Gunther, "She died in that hospital from both the infection and the lack of willpower to live."

His wife's death greatly affected Gunther, so much so that Karl told him, "Look, Gunther, you need to get away. Take off from work and rest awhile, pull yourself together."

"No, Uncle Karl," protested the young man. "I'm just like you and Dad. Got the same blood . . . Wallendas can't and don't quit."

Despite his words, another year ended on a tragic note.

Because of Margarita's fall, Karl needed another performer, so Dick reluctantly gave up his stint at home with Delilah and Tino and left the boat he loved to work on so that he could return to the Wallenda troupe to help Karl out, thinking it would be a temporary thing.

B y now, Delilah's only goal was to become a wirewalker like her mother and grandfather. She talked of little else, constantly asking her mother questions about performing in order to earn "brownie points" so that her mother would appreciate the seriousness of her desire. On one occasion

Delilah decided she'd show how dependable and mature she had become. Looking around for a task to impress her mother she spied her own badly scuffed shoes. She decided to polish them until they shone.

Avidly she tackled the job, her tongue sticking out the corner of her mouth as she concentrated on applying the coloring to the shoe. Then she began to shine them.

When she'd finished she proudly held up her saddlebacks in the air, a smile on her face. What a great job she'd done. Mommy would be so pleased now maybe she'd finally realize how grown-up Delilah was becoming.

The child moved the shoes to the side to admire them. Uh-oh. Right there, under the shoes, was a big glob of polish. All her grand plans evaporated. She knew her mother would be upset over the floor getting an unwanted dye job. She'd better clean it up. Methodically, young Delilah went to the sink, pulled a chair over and climbed on it to reach the running water. Rags, she needed rags. Well, towels would do. Maybe a bucket, too.

When Jenny walked up the trailer steps, Delilah was still kneeling on the floor washing the polish out. Jenny grabbed the door handle and yanked it open. Out gushed water.

"Oh, Delilah!" groaned her mother, who tiptoed in seeking dry land. "Oh, Delilah," Jenny said again, this time sounding as though she was totally exasperated. Grabbing some rags, Jenny got down on her hands and knees and started drying the floor which seemed to resemble a river.

This scene is a memory which has stayed with Delilah through the years. "She didn't yell or paddle me, because she knew my intentions were good," Delilah reflects. "She was a strict but loving and supportive mother who protected Tino and me from whatever dangers she perceived in our world and the world outside."

Delilah's comical attempts to show her seriousness about

becoming a circus performer went on and on. However, no matter what Delilah did, Jenny's husband Dick (whom Tino and Delilah called Uncle Dick) good naturedly accepted Delilah's antics. He loved both Delilah and her brother. He never made unrealistic demands on them, and always made himself available if Delilah or Tino needed him. To Delilah, he was "a very special guy." Compared to Jenny, however, he was not much of a disciplinarian.

For Delilah this was a stable period, with two parents and a brother around and security in knowing what her future goal was. Delilah was only six, but her sights were already focused strictly on walking the wire. Intently she watched her mother and Aunt Carla on the wire as they practiced alternating as the top-mounter in the seven-man pyramid. Because Aunt Carla was working too, Ricky often ended up in the company of his cousins Tino and Delilah. The three children played together, passing winter months with school and romping about. Delilah remembers Ricky as "always being up for something and ready to have fun. He was more rambunctious than Tino and I. Sometimes he was quick to anger. Once, when we were little, Ricky and I got into a fist fight over some stupid thing that kids get mad about. He and I were punching each other when all of a sudden he bit me, actually clamped his teeth over my skin. 'I can't believe it!' I told him. 'You fight dirty.' The childish fight was soon forgotten, however. At other times Ricky seemed kinder. We had fun. We were always together."

With Dick watching Delilah, her brother, and her cousin, Delilah began to handle her mother's absences better.

Sometimes when Jenny was on the road, Delilah was sent off to her father's, especially during the summers. There, Tino and she carried on as siblings do, sometimes getting along, while at other times scrapping.

During one of those summers when Delilah worked with

her father in one of his acts, she was taken to a doctor to receive one of her childhood immunizations. Twenty-four hours later her arm had blown up and was throbbing with pain. Her temperature shot up, too; it got higher as the day passed, and then still higher. She felt awful, but she didn't tell her father she was having a bad reaction to the shot. Instead she continued to work in the act, fearful of saying anything lest Alberto would make her go to bed and not perform, which was the most important thing to young Delilah.

It was about this time that Delilah sensed she was missing something. Even with all the Wallendas around, even with Tino and her parents there for her, and even with Dick's affection, she felt empty at times. She told Martha about it.

"Empty? Missing something?" responded her grandmother. "I know what you mean. You must look for the answer. It's right there in front of you." Martha had always been devoutly religious. She read the Bible to her grandchildren at dinner and she talked about God and what His place was in their lives. Martha's faith is strong. Delilah, however, was still a little girl and had endless questions. Who *was* this God? Was He someone as elusive as her parents? Would He give her the peace and direction she so badly wanted . . . *needed?* "I tell you," repeated Mutti Martha, "to find Him, you must go on your own search."

Why, Delilah wondered, was it so difficult for her? After all, Tino, who she knew had searched, too, seemed to have found God and established some secret relationship with Him. Why couldn't she be like Tino?

"I think I spent my entire childhood searching," syas Delilah. "It took a long time before I found the true answer."

* * *

59

What was not difficult, what she had known from the time she could stand on the lowwire, was that her life would be in the circus. At almost nine years old in 1961, Delilah began performing solos in public. Jenny had her doing the "Spanish Web." Delilah's first show was for the Tom Pax Circus. Jenny stood off to the side, watching her little girl perform like a pro. As the act neared its climax, Jenny was ready to scoop Delilah into her arms and tell her what a grand job she had done.

But then Jenny stiffened. Something was going wrong. Delilah's foot became tangled in the toe loop. Jenny looked to her side, seeing that the next act was ready to go on. "C'mon, Delilah. You've got to get down," she calls. But Delilah remained entangled. The audience quieted, aware that Delilah was stuck. Anxious minutes passed while Delilah freed herself. Spontaneously the audience broke into applause for the child as she walked, head held high, out of the ring.

Jenny knew then that Delilah was on her way. Besides performing, Delilah was active in other circus events. She and Tino sold snow cones or helped tear down the highwire when the Wallendas finished their act. They also did the opening parade for Jenny and Dick. The child's life became circus focused as she was caught up in practicing on the wire, doing somersaults on the trampoline, or taking her father's horse, Pasha, into the circus ring to trick-ride it. Her blood pumped wildly with the thrill of the big top.

Meanwhile, Karl was still excited about doing the seven-man, in spite of the fact that the family had been doing it for sixteen years. Other Wallendas, especially Herman, still felt that seven people on the wire at once with balancing poles and feet in the way could be dangerous. Nevertheless Karl persisted with his dream to make this act one to beat all, prompting Herman to comment, "Karl is afraid of dying in bed."

For Karl, the biggest problem was finding replacements for those understanders who quit. And they did quit. Some were scared, others found better jobs with bigger circuses, and a few left because all the traveling was too hard on their families.

Even at her tender age, Delilah knew she would become one of them, performing stunts that amazed people. Already she could feel the urgency of her desire to be on the wire pumping through her. Everything and everyone in her life was "circus." Because her own desire to be one of the Wallendas was so intense, she wondered why so many people, especially for the "seven," came and went much the same way a revolving door spins.

She finally asked her grandfather, "Why do so many people you train leave the 'seven'?"

Vati looked about wistfully and shrugged. "Lots of reasons," he began. "Some fall in love, some fall out; others go on to do their own wire acts, and still others are not made to do the 'seven' and so they shouldn't be up there with us who are."

Delilah understood.

What she didn't understand was why her grandfather lamented the very act that had made him renowned. "Because," he tried to tell her, "replacements are always hard to find, and the act costs more than it makes. If I find a man to replace a quitter and he's married, then I have to take care of his wife and children, plus pay their travel and other expenses. My paycheck gets so thinned out that after I'm done paying off the performers, there's little left for me or for the rest of the family."

"Then why do it?" she persisted.

"Ah," he said, "it's beautiful, and no one else in the world can do it. We're the only ones, the best in the whole world. The 'seven' is making us famous."

But it wasn't just *seven* of them anymore; now there were nine performers: one stood at the end of the platform and handed the chair to the top-mounter, and another stood at the opposite platform to take off the chair.

Throughout this period Vati had to rely on his performers to do the act faithfully every time it was rendered. Not one change could be made without it encroaching on everyone on the wire; not the slightest cold could be tolerated by any one performer without it threatening the lives of all; not one error by a sole rigger could be made without it menacing each of the seven.

Awed, Delilah told herself, "Just think about it, every time you climb the wire, your coming out alive rests on other people's competence."

Needing strong bodies to replace those wirewalkers who quit the act, Karl considered what untapped relatives might yet be available. This idea came to him about the same time Berlin was being walled off, sharply defining Germany's split into East and West, communist and free. Many prople wanted to flee East Germany in hopes of shaking off the restrictions placed upon them. Lottie Schepp and her children, Dieter and Jana, were one of those families who existed in a walled-in country where free will and free expression were no longer tolerated.

Dieter, Mutti Martha's twenty-two-year-old nephew, resented getting out of bed every morning in a land where a wall restrained his mind, restricted his choices, and limited his actions. He wanted to vault the Berlin Wall into West Germany.

Although Karl no longer was related to Martha Wallenda Henderson since he had long ago divorced her, he nonetheless felt attached to her and her kin because they once had been family; and to Karl, family was family no matter how many chains had been snapped over time. So when Dieter showed up at Karl's office trailer while the Wallenda troupe was performing in West Germany, Karl was pleased. In German, he asked the lad, "How is it you are here when you are impounded in East Germany?"

"I escape, Uncle Karl; I make it over the wall."

The two men laughed and clasped each other's shoulders.[10]

How Dieter actually escaped has never been learned; Karl always refused to discuss it. Nonetheless, Vati was very impressed with Dieter's courage and he needed to add people to his act. So Karl turned Dieter into an understander in the human seven-man pyramid. And he decided Dieter's sixteen-year-old sister Jana, who was christened Christina and was petite and nimble, would make a good replacement for Carla (who had left the pyramid to work in her husband's act) or for Jenny, who needed someone to alternate with as top-mounter.

"But," Jenny observed on hearing about the addition of Jana and Dieter, "our troupe has never had this many."[11]

"Ja," admitted Karl.

His wife Helen added, "The seven-man is dangerous for any number of people."

Karl nodded, but he was committed to the act. And now, with new replacements, nothing could stop him.

"We'll be rich," said Dieter, grinning at the prospect. "This is America."

"Nobody gets rich in the circus, even in America," warned Karl.

Although Jana and Dieter were eager to get to work and mine the mythical gold lining America's streets, their mother Lottie was less enthusiastic. She went to Karl and heatedly proclaimed, "You fill my children's heads with big promises. It's dangerous, what you want from them, to walk a little wire so high up in the air."

"Aw, no worry there. All we Wallendas do it," Karl countered, brushing off her criticism. He laughingly added, "You fret too much, Lottie; everything'll be fine."

And so in no time, Martha was reunited with her sister-in-law, niece, and nephew—both of whom worked daily at mastering the wire.

For Delilah, her German cousins proved interesting. Watching them, she says, she saw "how hard the Schepps practiced for the 'seven.' I never thought Dieter liked it as much as the others. Uncle Mario never complained about doing it, nor did Dick or Uncle Gunther. Yet Dieter seemed always to be whining and grousing about how sore he was after practice. So while I was going on with my life as a child, the adults were going on with their lives performing the pyramid. What I remember most about these practices is how everyone in the family kept telling Dieter not to throw his pole in the air because he might not catch it."

More days passed, filled with more practices. Delilah took it all in. She noticed Dieter still had problems with the wire. Delilah never failed to attend their rehearsals, enjoying hearing Vati take control, telling people how to do this, ordering them to do that—because he was the expert and they were not. She listened to her grandfather regularly barking at Dieter, "Hold your pole up. Don't let it lean to one side, and never, ever, ever drop it. You understand, Dieter? Never ever drop your pole! Never toss it into the air and try to catch it!"

Always Dieter nodded.

"People are depending on you, Dieter. Never throw the pole," ordered Karl.

"Ja," Dieter responded. "I understand."

Absorbed, Delilah also noticed that in spite of endless

practices, Jana didn't perform as well as Jenny, and Dieter still wasn't getting the hang of it. She heard her uncle Mario say to Vati that he had doubts about Dieter. But her grandfather only responded, "He'll be fine, Mario; you'll see."

Weeks later, with her back against a tree, Delilah gazed up at the wire; the seven moved across the cable like a colossal slug, step by step, breath by breath, each of their muscles pulsing synchronously with one another. She thought Dieter was finally coming through, even though he was still shaky on the wire. Sweat gathered at his forehead, temple, arms, down his cheeks. The amount of concentration he expended worried Delilah. She held her breath until the seven reached the end of the wire and stepped onto the platform, where they were safe. Then she let it out.

How was it, she wondered, that they stayed balanced up there with each of them hooked to one another: Dieter leading the pack, with Dick yoked to him; behind Dick, Mario yoked to Gunther. On the next row up was Uncle Herman collared to Vati, and on the third level was her mother sitting in the chair she climbed atop whenever the slug got to the middle of the wire. Delilah trembled, wondering at their bravery. Were they born that way? From the top down she stared at each one in turn, and then her gaze fastened on Dieter. Certainly he was brave—after all, he'd fled from communist East Germany, took his life in his own hands— but he was not born into the circus. Could the spectators tell that?

She knew her family could because their concern remained. Periodically, they protested again: "Dieter's still not sure on the wire." But Vati only replied, "Relax. I've trained all of you; I can train them. I can train anyone. Besides, people are always nervous about new performers."

Delilah studied Dieter's face as he crossed the wire, the eyes of the slug, the first one out to get the view of the world before him. If he was the slug's eyes, then Grandfather must be the slug's brain, and Mommy the slug's antennae. But Dieter didn't seem to be enjoying the panorama his position gave him. Actually, she thought, he looked as though he was in pain, with his eyes squinting, a frown curling his lips, sweat streaming over his cheeks, his teeth clenched. She'd wanted to ask him why he looked so unhappy up there. She'd heard one of the grown-ups say that Dieter really wanted to stay in Florida to lay tile but he was doing the wire because he felt he owed Karl a year of work. She watched Dieter more intently; to her he didn't look like a wirewalker.

But look! He was smiling now! They'd all reached the platform at the other end of the wire where they stood chatting among themselves, slapping each other's backs and saying, "Wonderful!" "Good job!" Now they were all smiling and discussing in loud, electrified voices what they could do to improve upon what they'd already done so well. Delilah stood below them, listening, watching, and feeling as though her lungs would burst from anxiety. Would she ever be able to do what they did—what the Wallendas had done for generations?

Vati was standing on the platform looking down at her, waving. She motioned with her small hand, smiled . . . breathed again. Oh, to be just like them! She would have to practice on the wire the way they did so that some day she too would be a famous highwire walker . . . if only she didn't get airsick up there, or just plain sick from being scared. She already had some accomplishments: doing the web act, at other times performing in her father's dog act, or marching in parades. Still, she hadn't walked the wire like them. Nevertheless, the little she has practiced on it has only served to increase her desire to perform. Since she turned nine this month—December—she would be old enough to go on the road with them for their next performance. Yet she knew being nine didn't carry enough power to convince her mother to let her do anything, let alone ride to Detroit with them for the seven-man act.

"It's just a regular performance," said Jenny, when Delilah begged to come along. "We've been doing it for sixteen years. No big deal."

"But I've been watching all of you practice. And I want to see Dieter and Jana do it in front of an audience."

"You go to school and that's that," her mother answered.

For Delilah the months she was doomed to remain in school seemed like a death sentence to her, but particularly agonizing was having to stay back in Sarasota while the clan went off to Michigan to perform the pyramid in the Shrine Circus on January 29th. Since she couldn't go, she felt they all shouldn't go; after all, Vati would turn fifty-seven and you'd think he'd want to stay home to celebrate his birthday. But oh no; they were off to Detroit to perform while Delilah had to stay with Mutti Martha.

Delilah asked her mother, "What's it like being at the tip-top of the human triangle, up so high and all alone?"

Jenny shrugged, looking at her daughter. "It's just an act."

"But you could fall . . . and die," she whispered.

"And I could die in bath water." Then she smiled at her child. "It's what I do for a living—the only thing I've ever really done. The 'seven' has gone on for years without the slightest accident. We're professionals, and being that, we take risks. It is our job, our life—as natural as our breathing is. Some day you too will be performing high on the wire." She gave the child a hug. "There's nothing to worry about."

Delilah agonized all the same. What if just one time when her mother so gallantly climbed the chair, rode it to the middle of the wire, and then stood on it . . . she fell? How many feet? A hundred, wasn't it? After all, she was fifteen feet higher than the six people below her. Any of them could have a bad day. People did make mistakes.

The next day, Delilah again watched them practice. Dieter was complaining again. This time he said his calves hurt, his hands were blistered and calloused. Maybe Dieter just wasn't made to do the pyramid, and yet she'd heard her grandfather say that he "broke Dieter in good," and that "the boy has no fears, and holds like a rock." Surely Dieter would perform wonderfully. But what if Vati was wrong this one time? She told herself over and over not to worry. But she couldn't seem to stop.

SIX

Precarious Flight

Karl's older brother Herman observed:

> Certainly we're afraid, but you must always feel safe up
> there. If you don't feel afraid, then, either you're a fool
> or you haven't got enough experience. You don't want
> anyone up there who is not afraid. It's not over until [we
> reach the platform]. The possibility of [an] accident ex-
> its in our minds and we accept the fact. . . . We all
> know our time will come. . . . We live with the philoso-
> phy of predestination. . . . He [God] knows when,
> where, and how you come and when, where, and how
> you go. . . . I've never had a premonition that kept me
> from going up. If I ever do, then I'm out of show busi-
> ness.[12]

Karl agreed with Herman, "An inexperienced person can
bring us [all] down." But for some reason, Karl mentally
buried that thought before he and his troupe left for Detroit
for their January 1962 seven-man booking.

A few evenings before they left, the family sat around talking about the Detroit trip, not in their normally excited way

but in a quietly worried way. They talked about how long the trip was and how everyone would feel tired and drained, and whether they'd run into snow, making the roads difficult to travel, and how much higher than usual the wire would be strung. And then they became silent, each absorbed in his or her own thoughts. The troupe—Jenny, Gunther, Herman, Dick, Mario, Karl, and Mike—seemed unusually concerned to Delilah. Of course, Jana and Dieter would also be there, along with Marga, Fontaine, and Marty. But Vati reassured everyone that this show, like the others, would be a gigantic success.

"I tell you what," he said to his family. "I won't let Dieter carry the pyramid the first week, okay? Ja?" This seemed to soothe the anxious troupe, but not Delilah, who picked up subtle signs that no one really wanted to do this engagement.

Before leaving for Detroit, Dick told Jenny, "I've put a deposit on a boat." He shrugged, adding, "You know how much I want to be around boats."

Jenny understood that he didn't want to work the wire anymore and she accepted this, although she'd surely miss his being with her all the time.

"I'll do the Detroit engagement, but then I want to work on my boat."

The day the trailers hit the road for Detroit, Delilah and Tino went to Mutti Martha's to stay. Michigan was a long drive from Sarasota, over a thousand miles, and even though Vati had traveled throughout his career, he still couldn't get over America's vastness. The touring seemed to wear on him more each year.

Delilah watched the caravan pull away. Sadly, her eyes filled with unexplainable tears.

Many hours later, the Wallendas arrived at Michigan State

Fairgrounds safely, albeit bushed and restless. The next day they rehearsed.

Although in practice Dieter appeared to have mastered his job in the pyramid, he still seemed unnatural on the wire. Still, the troupe said little since Karl promised them that he wouldn't let Dieter carry the pyramid the first week. Although no one could find fault with Dieter's performance, outside of his protesting about how hard the work was on his muscles and how exhausted he was after the trip, he still made everyone a little nervous. The troupe shrugged off his bellyaching because the wire was gruelling for apprentices, requiring sturdy and enduring bones, powerful muscles, deep concentration, and steady nerves. Vati reassured him, "Fine, Dieter, you did fine in practice," knowing that the boy was young and in time he too, like all the others, would become an ace on the wire, limber in balancing and adroit at handling the pole.

Opening night arrived. The troupe climbed to the platform. Jenny was the top-mounter for the night, and Jana would take her turn the next day. To everyone's surprise, Dieter was up there, too; Karl had changed his mind. Vati kept his eyes trained on the lad throughout the entire twelve minutes of the act. But Dieter appeared alert, intently listening to Gunther's directions, moving in rhythm with everyone else on the wire.

The applause began before they reached the platform. Dieter stepped off the wire first, a big smile on his face. Everyone grinned, breathing a little easier, relieved that the worst part was over. The troupe followed Dieter off the wire and onto the platform to take their bows, and immediately they were greeted by thundering applause that echoed throughout the arena, slamming of hands together—noise they had come to recognize as appreciation. Each of them basked in it. Applause for them was a high. They relaxed, feeling that once the opening-night performance was through, the next day's matinee would go off without a hitch.

However, late that night, Jenny woke from a horrific nightmare. In it, the troupe's third performance at Detroit didn't go as planned. The performers ran out into their spotlight, climbed the wire, waving and smiling at the audience, and started out with Dieter taking the first step on the wire. Smugly and confidently they slid along the cable, feeling good about their abilities. Then all of a sudden the worst happened—they were falling. Jenny jerked awake and tried to shake off the atrocity. "It's a dream," she told herself. "Only a vision, nothing more."

She awoke early the next day, feeling a little tired, but glad the vision of disaster was behind her. Jana took Jenny's place for the matinee. The performance went off without a snag, and loud applause rang out. What was Jenny worried about? Dieter had come through, just as her father expected. In fact, Dieter's handling of the pole was better than the previous night's act when he seemed a little jittery. Dieter, however, said nothing, and that perhaps troubled the troupe more than any display of cockiness. But Karl exhibited no consternation; he was just pleased that his troupe was intact, no one was quitting, and big arenas were booking his seven-man pyramid.

Sometime late in the day, Jana told Jenny, "I'll top-mount tonight."

Jenny pulled back, surprised. "Why? It's my turn. You did it at the matinee."

But Jana persisted. "No, I want to do it; it's important to me."

Jenny looked around, then back at the youngster. "Whatever."

The rest of the day passed quickly. Dick, Gunther, and Jenny got a bite to eat, dallied, and played endless pranks on each other. Soon they found themselves only a few hours away from the evening show. Jenny went over to Jana, who was off to the side looking pale and sweaty. Suddenly Jana went into a swoon and collapsed.

When she came to, Jenny asked worriedly, "What's the matter? You scared?"

"I have a stomach ache."

"Did you eat? You have to eat to perform well. Do you have money to eat?"

Jana shook her head. "I used my money to buy make-up."

"You mean you didn't eat at all today?" At once Jenny got Jana some food and said, "I'll top-mount tonight like I'm supposed to. You sit and watch until you feel better."

"But I am better."

"You passed out."

"But I'm fine now that I ate." Jana persisted. "Either I do it or I quit."

Jenny gave in to her.

Throughout their encounter, Dieter was dealing with problems of his own. A head cold coupled with complete exhaustion had him down. Not only was he tired from the rigors of the act, but he was also moonlighting as a propman in order to make more money.

"What's wrong, Dieter?" Gunther asked.[13]

"Nothing, just tired."

Gunther then went up to Karl. "Dieter's saying he's sick. Maybe you should talk to him."

Karl nodded and began looking for Dieter, but with all Karl had to do he didn't find Dieter until right before the evening performance. Then the two stood talking when Karl noticed the canvas banner behind Dieter announcing a motorcycle act. On it was painted a skull and crossbones—the death head.

"I'm fine, Uncle Karl."

Karl replied softly, "You're sure? Be honest. If not, Mike can take your place." Mike was a regular substitute for the Wallenda troupe because he was familiar with the seven-man; when not on the wire, he stood on a pedestal and put the top-mounter's chair on the bar. Dieter's spot on the wire was as dangerous as any other person in the "seven," but Karl had made a point of assigning him the front position because his view was least obstructed.

Dieter added, "I don't even have a sniffle, let alone a full-blown cold. You and Uncle Herman worry too much." Then he was off to join the rest of the troupe.

But today, three decades later, sixty-four-year-old Gunther doesn't recall that exchange taking place. "I don't remember saying anything to Karl about Dieter being sick, but I could have. And I don't remember Karl and Dieter ever having that conversation. My cousin Jenny, though, does recollect that Dieter had a cold." Gunther, who often reflects on his life as a famous highwire Wallenda, has over the years thought deeply about what happened and thus formed his own views.

As if on second thought, Gunther, who's walked the wire since age five, adds, "You know, when we first did the 'seven' only experienced wirewalkers were in it, but then as Karl found it hard to replace those who quit he had to rely on inexperienced men, some who never walked the wire before and had to be trained just for the 'seven.' When we did Detroit, it was our first time up high at 36 feet; before that, we had only practiced at 10 and 20 feet."

That night in Detroit, Gunther and Jenny talked to each other as they got ready to go on stage. Jenny took note that her father was protesting about the length of his costume pants—a sure sign of nervousness and so unlike him—and he went to Marga to have them fixed. Still, although everyone seemed edgy, nothing out of the ordinary was happening. Everyone dressed and chatted among themselves.

"Everyone ready?" Karl called out, checking his watch. He gathered his brood and the nine of them—Karl, Herman, Gunther, Mario, Dick, Dieter, Jana, Jenny, and Mike—left for the arena where they saw the wire stretched, as always, 49 feet from pedestal to pedestal and 36 feet off the ground, with no net below.

Off to the side, the troupe stood watching the act before them finish to a round of clapping. Periodically Jenny glanced at Jana, and Gunther at Dieter, but nothing seemed amiss. The performers looked magnificent in their sparkling, jewel-colored costumes accenting their lean, spry bodies and their fair Teutonic coloring. Karl and his troupe now stood at the arena's entrance, waiting to be announced.

"And now, ladies and gentlemen, for an act that has thrilled audiences for years everywhere, an act yet to be duplicated, I present Theeeeee Great Wallendas!" cried the ringmaster with a flourish of his hand toward the performers.

The spotlight flashed on them; Karl grinned widely, seeming pleased with all he had accomplished over the years, pleased with how far he had come from wobbling chairs in a beer garden for a few measly rubles back in Germany. As if by signal, the troupe extended their right arms in greeting and smiled. Then off they ran to the highwire. As each climbed the platform, the lights went out in the arena except for the spot-beams on the troupe. Their first stunts went off without a snag.

Then came the famous drum roll, and the ringmaster's voice boomed, "Pa-leeeese, everyone must be quiet. The nature of this act requires absolute silence." Like children in a classroom, the spectators become still.

The giant slug began forming. Mike McGuire stood on a

pedestal that was higher than the other platform, and placed a chair atop the top bar for Jana to sit on. With him on the stand were Jenny and Fontaine. At the other end of the wire, Marty would remove the chair as the pyramid eased toward her platform.

As the sound of "Evening Star" echoed throughout the large arena,[14] Gunther called, "Easy out," the famous words associated with the Wallendas' performance. The slug began to slide out onto the wire when Dieter's leather ballet-like slipper touched the first spot of metal. The slug was in motion, balancing poles see-sawing as the creature glided across the wire.

Karl talked gently to the troupe. "Easy boys." To Dieter he cautioned, "Gently, gently." The members' positions on the pyramid were the same as in their practices. On the bottom, Gunther was in the rear—the hardest stance for any understander, because Gunther couldn't see in front of him. The jolt he had to endure when the seven artists first left the platform was enough to up-end him. But Gunther, next to his father and uncle, was the most expert, so he served in the tail-end position. Harnessed to Gunther and in front of him was Mario. Dick, who was hitched to Dieter, stood in front of Mario. On the next level up, Herman stood on the yoked bar between his son Gunther and Mario. Herman was fastened to Karl, who stood on the collared bar between Dick and Dieter. The front man had to lean back to hold the pyramid while the rear man had to push forward. And on the top row was Jana, alone. She was sitting on a chair on the bar hooked between Herman and Karl, her legs wrapped around the legs of the chair, and in her lap was her own long balancing pole.

The slug made its way to the center of the wire. The men stood perfectly still as Jana began to rise to rest her bottom against the back of the chair. Karl talked softly to the team.

Sweat rolled down their faces. Their utterly immobile stances were difficult to maintain, as Jana's movements slightly jarred their balance: The weight on their shoulders was almost unbearable. The poles got heavier the longer the performers were on the wire, especially when they neared the opposite platform. To alleviate the pole's weight, pros knew enough to curl their wrists while holding it, but Dieter didn't seem to do this. The eyes of the seven performers remained fixed on an arbitrary spot in front of them while Jana painfully pulled her legs up to press against the seat of the chair—all in slow, deliberate strokes. Quivering, she managed to stand, if only briefly. Her trembling could be detected by spectators who were frozen, watching.

"Jana, you all right? You standing?" Karl asked, though neither he nor the troupe needed to look; the audience's gasped, oohs and aahs and cheers spoke the answer. Then the room became absolutely quiet again. "Good, good," Karl encouraged delicately, softly. In the hush, viewers could hear him speak.

Karl saw only directly ahead; he looked at Marty on the platform, waiting for her to signal. Marty watched Jana, then she nodded that "yes," Jana was fine. Jana above him moved into position; she moved once again and sat down, and then her weight laid upon his shoulders. Next, she said, "Ready"—she was set to move. The few claps that broke through the quiet were immediately silenced by other bystanders.

The major part of the act was over, but the most dangerous was yet to come—the part that made high wirewalkers tense, the segment they dreaded the most. Yet there was no other way . . . they had to wirewalk their way to the platform at the opposite end. They could not turn around and retrace their steps. And they couldn't just stand on the wire

forever; they had to go forward, had to brave the most perilous part of the stunt.

"Don't relax," insisted Karl while they were on the wire.
"Keep alert until you reach the ground." Too often the
troupe became elated prematurely, which would make them
eager to finish the stunt so they could reach the platform and
receive their well-deserved accolades. But this eagerness
could create a carelessness in their critical trek across the
remainder of the wire. Karl had told them a thousand times
not to become reckless and hurry to the end after the top-
mounter returned to her seat.

All seemed to go well. Dieter was taking nice slow steps in
sync with the others on the wire. Everyone was beginning to
relax.

"Slowly ahead," chimed Gunther.

Just a few more moments on the wire and it would be
over, this daredevil antic, the most hazardous in the history
of circus stunts, the most excruciating trick any troupe had
ever done.

There was less than ten feet to go. Karl was perspiring
badly . . . and he had done this act dozens and dozens of
times before. He could not but wonder what Dieter must
have been feeling; certainly he too was sweating. Was he
aware of the deadly tranquility in the arena? Did it bother
him? Not everyone could handle having all those eyes focused on them; was Dieter like that? Maybe too self-con-
scious? This trick required painstaking concentration,
nerves mighty as steel cables, muscles of herculean strength.

The 'seven' act was draining; anything could go wrong on
the highwire. It wouldn't take much to topple the seven: A
photographer's bulb could disrupt one of the understander's
concentration, or the maddening and stifling heat on the
wire at the top of the big top could make any of the seven
pass out. Sudden noises such as lightning or audience

shouts were another concern, since they could disengage performers and cause them to lose their balance. Also, sheer, intense fear could suddenly assault even a veteran, and then it would all be over within seconds. People had been known to crack on the wire, just go to pieces without warning. Twelve minutes wasn't a long time, but on the wire it was an eternity.

Now they were almost at the opposite platform, where Marty waited. Almost over . . . so why was Karl so uptight this time? Why this uneasiness incubating in him? His eyes tried to take in everyone on the wire, but his vision was limited by his position on the wire. Nothing seemed to be out of place, yet he was afraid everything was not in place. Relax, he told himself. It's almost done, and when it's over, the cheers will come and the seven will descend the wire filled with glee and self-praise.

Yet he couldn't seem to shake the feeling that something was wrong. He felt it so strongly at the moment, but he couldn't put his finger on what it was. Less than three feet. Karl's eyes focused on Marty's face. Her expression was the same as always. Soon she'd get into position to reach out and take the chair off the bar, and *voila*, the act would be done. Then another night would pass and the next day they'd psyche themselves up again to perform the same stunt, again. Less than a minute to go to reach the platform.

Then something moved.

Immediately Karl perceived it. What kind of motion? he wondered. Unnatural. Like a tiny current signalling an oncoming flood. Fear swept through him. He stiffened while trying to locate the source of the vibration. "Steady, steady," he called out, as though his words would reverse the frightening waft of air passing over him.

Then the slug faltered, just a tiny bit, not enough for anyone in the audience to notice but enough to scare the hell out of the performers. "Easy," Karl said again, his voice sounding raspy. Something was askew! He lowered his eyes toward Dieter, but he couldn't see plainly because of all the balancing poles. Vati kept his eyes riveted toward the boy, wondering if he was the problem, the cause of the movement. Then he abruptly saw, a split-second too late, that Dieter's pole listed oddly to one side.

"Dieter," Karl called softly. "You all right? Straighten your pole."

Silence.

Karl noticed how heavily his performers were breathing and yet how shallow it sounded, as if taking long breaths would disrupt the moment—a moment in time when no one knew for sure what was wrong and yet everyone sensed that all would come apart.

"Dieter?" Karl called. In German he asked, "What's the matter?"

Then he heard something: Dieter mumbling, talking to himself. No one ever did that in formation, because it cut through concentration—a concentration that had to be steady and profound, for lives depended on it.

Karl studied Dieter, whose pole dipped even more. "Dieter!" Karl cried. Then, to all the performers, Vati the maestro barked, "Keep going! We have only a few steps left."

His eyes met Marty's, and in her eyes he saw his own fear reflected back at him. Certainly everyone must know now; his only hope was that the pyramid would stay together for the few remaining paces to the platform.

Suddenly, Dieter jostled the pole into the air—perhaps in an attempt to ease the weight on his hands.

Karl sucked his breath, knowing what happened when a wirewalker let go of his only source of balance . . . even if only for a heartbeat.

The wire shuddered.

Suddenly Dieter wailed the words that would echo around the world: "I can't hold it any longer!" He let the pole roll out of his fingers. It plummeted to the floor, where it uncannily bounced before settling deadly still on the ground.

The performers were frozen still for one more deadly second, and then they crumbled the way a building topples in an earthquake.

As Dieter and Dick went down, Gunther felt his shoulder slack, but his eyes missed the bodies tumbling through the air. In the outburst of screams and shrieks, he looked around and saw his father and uncle oddly twisted, grasping the wire.

He was the only one standing on the wire with the balancing pole. Without considering the high degree of danger to himself, Gunther swung into motion, 36 feet off the ground, trying to save three lives.

His uncle, he quickly determined, had whacked into steel rigging that gashed deep into his thigh as he clung to the wire with both hands, his foot ensnared in guy wires. Next Gunther's eyes took in his father, who hung from the wire with both hands. And down below lay Dick, Dieter, and Mario . . . perfectly still.

No time to think about that, for Jana and her chair were whizzing past. Flying through the air, a split second later, the chair free-fell on Mario while Jana slammed into Karl, slicing him farther into the steel cable. The second she hit him, Jana turned mad. She tore at him, trying to find a handle on his body to stop her from falling, hitting the hard floor, ending up lying lifeless next to her brother. Her weight caused Karl to sink farther below the wire; it was all he could do to hold on.

Gunther saw that his uncle's wedged foot prevented him from crossing the wire hand-over-hand to the platform, so he started across the cable with his pole. Vati moaned; hearing him, Gunther realized Karl's pain must be incredible—being split into two—but the 57-year-old man still fought to clutch Jana, despite the wire cutting deep into his flesh.

"Don't let me go!" screamed Jana. "Please don't drop me!" she screeched pathetically, her fear so real, it was palpable.

Through gnashed teeth, Karl bellowed, "God help me, Jana, if I leave my leg up here, I won't let you go!"

Gunther worked his way over to his father, all the while shaking his head and muttering, "Christ almighty! It happened, really happened."[15] A shiver ran through him. "Dad, I've still got my pole; are you okay?" he asked Herman, who had a big gash in his forehead from falling into the wire.

"I'm fine. I can make it to the platform. Get your uncle."

"I'm stepping over you; watch your hands," said Gunther as he walked away from his father and toward his uncle. In the background, the howling and sobbing raged, but Gunther kept his attention riveted on Karl and Jana. She was beginning to slip from him.

Instantly, Gunther was at Karl's side, reaching down to ease Jana off his back, but the girl was frantic, gripping and pulling Vati so hard that she was sure to yank him down with her. Jana was petite, weighing less than 100 pounds, yet she felt like a lead safe—too heavy for Gunther, who felt weak and unsteady himself, to pull her up on the wire and across it to the platform. He knew what he had to do; a look passed between him and his uncle. In seconds, Gunther—with his pole at an angle near him—grappled with Jana until he finally stripped her off Karl, who turned and grabbed her other hand. The two held the teenager by her wrists while men on the ground arranged a makeshift safety net.

"Oh God, no! Don't let me go!" she screeched, now understanding their plans.

"You'll be okay," Gunther said in the most persuasive tone he could muster.

Jana wailed louder, "Don't drop me! For God's sake, don't drop me!" Her cries pierced the tension as thick as an iron curtain.

"Jana," Gunther said, his knees shaking. Below, he saw Dick, Jenny's husband, try like an injured deer to lift his head but just as quickly collapse again. "Jana, don't struggle," said Gunther. "Try to land in a sitting position and not on your feet. Don't land on your feet!"

She cried, "Oh dear God, help me."

Gunther and Karl counted out loud: "One . . ."

"Remember, land in a sitting position," Gunther said quickly.

"Two . . ."

"Please, please, hold me, don't let me go!"

"Three!" They released their grasp, and down she fell like a missile, straight into the net made of riding mats. Men who clenched the mat—there were no handholds on the vinyl—felt their hands slipping the second Jana slapped down. She landed feet-first and immediately bounced out and hit the solid, packed-dirt floor.

Gunther glanced over at his father, who was monkey-walking his way across the wire to the platform. Seeing that he was safe, Gunther turned his attention back to his uncle. "Is it bad?" he asked.

Karl, who was near unconsciousness from pain, nodded.

Summoning his last strength, Gunther helped Karl to the nearest platform—the one where Marty stood, horrified. Vati was breathless by the time she could help get him safely on the stand.

Karl shouted between gasps, "Gunther, Herman, go down and see if the boys are all right."

At first Gunther looked strangely at his uncle, and then he

realized Karl had no idea what had really happened. He said nothing to the master. Nor did he descend to learn of his three comrades' fate. Instead, he focused on his cousin Jenny, who sat curled on the platform, hands glued to the railing.

"Jenny," he called, lifting the balancing pole and heading across the wire.

Jenny stared straight ahead, numbed.

"Someone get her down," Gunther said.

For Jenny, whose terror made her body go rigid, the only thing of significance to her now was her husband. Somehow she had to get down from the platform and run to Dick, whom she saw lying motionless on the ground. Frenzied, her mind searched for the rope to descend, but frightened and confused, she couldn't find it. *Where was the rope? Why wasn't it there like it always was? What happened to it?* The thought flashed fleetingly that she should just "go down," but no sooner had the idea streaked through her mind than Mike was beside her, tying a rope around her to hoist her to the ground.

As Gunther watched Jenny being lowered, his eyes caught sight of his father helping Vati down the rope ladder. He followed his father's path. Now all the Wallendas were on the ground. The second Jenny reached the floor, she screamed, "My husband!" She ran toward him. Police and Shrine officials encircled Dieter, Dick, and Mario, preventing her from getting through. She pressed toward the center of the arena where they lay, but hands from everywhere pulled her back.

SEVEN

Fate's Fickle Fingers

At the hospital, Jenny and Gunther sat together, knowing there was security in familiar and loving faces. They awaited word of the fate of Dick, Dieter, Mario, Jana, and Karl. Back in the arena, the circus had already returned to full swing. The center ring where the Wallendas had fallen had been cleared. Upbeat music was playing, clowns were tumbling. It was on with the show.

In the waiting area of the hospital, however, a darker mood prevailed. Jenny said to Gunther, "No word?"

Shaking his head sadly, Gunther replied quietly, "None of the boys have regained consciousness." He put an arm around his cousin.

Jenny buried her head in her hands. They continued waiting. The halls were filling with reporters. Down the hall, a plethora of noises—countless medical personnel rushed in and out of the emergency room, machines were wheeled in and out, bells and buzzers sounded.

Inside the room a doctor approached Karl, who was struggling to get out of bed, "You must keep still, Mr. Wallenda. I'm going to have to hospitalize you; you're badly injured with a double hernia and a cracked pelvis."

"Is my son all right?" Karl asked hoarsely.

No one answered.

"He is alive?" Karl saw nurses and physicians exchanging furtive looks. "He's alive, isn't he?" His voice rose, struck high teetering notes.

Still no response.

As soon as the medical personnel were distracted, Karl limped out into the hallway, looking for the boys who had fallen. Limping down the corridor, his hand braced the wall for support. He peered through windows of private cubicles. He grabbed a nurse: "My son, Mario Wallenda . . . where is he?"

The nurse pointed to a room further down the hall.

Karl passed room after room until he saw a form lying on a Stryker frame. Warily, the once-confident, strong patriarch entered the silent cubicle.

His son lay in a steel bed, his skull fractured. "Mario, Mario," whispered Karl, his voice breaking. Karl saw that his son was comatose. *Is he paralyzed?* Vati asked himself. *He must be if his skull and neck are damaged.* Karl wept.

A doctor and a nurse entered. "Mr. Wallenda," began the doctor, "you must choose. Your son is badly hurt; his spinal cord was crushed and he has severe head injuries. You must make a decision. We can operate right now so that he might not be paralyzed but might yet die in surgery, or we can wait and leave him paralyzed but not die. You need to decide now."

Karl looked at the medical man, studied his eyes; then his gaze moved to his son. How could they ask Karl to make such a choice? Should he try to restore his son's health and risk killing him, or give him life but condemn him to an eternity of dead legs? Karl shook his head, biting his lip. He had always made decisions quickly and easily before, but now he couldn't even decide if he wanted to stand or sit, let alone make a sound judgment about his son's existence. Long seconds passed before he announced, "I want him alive. Don't operate."

Karl left his son's room, still sobbing. From a distance, he spotted his daughter sitting out in the hall waiting with Herman and Gunther. He wondered what they were waiting for. Then he realized they were anticipating news about Dick, Dieter, and Jana. Karl wiped away his tears and approached his daughter.

"Jenny," he said brokenly. "My Jenny." He went toward her.

She looked at him searchingly, and then she turned her head. He walked nearer to her. Still she ignored him.

He had opened his mouth to speak when he heard a reporter come down the hall and yell, "Hey! Who's Jenny Wallenda? Her husband just died."

Shocked, Jenny jumped up, lunged at the reporter, attacking him, screaming, "Liar! Liar!" Gunther quickly got up and pulled his cousin off the insensitive man.

"Jenny," he admonished through clenched teeth. "Calm down, let him go." And yet Gunther too would have liked to slam his fist into the reporter's face.

"Let him go, Jenny," implored Gunther. But Jenny was mad—crazy with grief and anguish—and no amount of pleading with her was going to quiet her. When she didn't, Gunther swiftly brought his hand across her cheek; the crack rang out.

The instant he hit her, she pulled back, numbed, and stared at him.

He embraced her; guided her to a chair. Moments later, he announced, "I'll be back," and headed for the phone.

Karl sat down next to Jenny, trying to talk to his daughter.

At the pay phone, Gunther found he had no pockets in his costume and hence no money. Somehow, a coin seemed to magically appear in the return box and he dropped it into the slot. He dialed the number, his hands shaking. "Are you sitting?" he asked when Helen answered the phone. "We came down."

Helen's voice wobbled, "Mario? Karl? How are they?"

"Please be calm," he said.

"Karl?"

"His hip."

"Mario?" Helen's voice was so near frenzy that Gunther was fearful of saying anything more. "How's Mario?"

"He's unconscious."

Silence.

Gunther wet his lips, then went on. "Dieter was dead on arrival," he said sadly. "Dick just died. Jana was shaken up pretty bad; they're doing tests."

The sounds Helen made at the other end were eerie, unnatural, keening the air.

Minutes later, Gunther replaced the phone on the hook, not sure how he had ended the conversation or what Helen had said or done. It took him a while before he got his feet moving and walked back to the waiting area to be with his cousin, father, uncle . . . and all those reporters.

A formidable-looking stranger approached him. "Mr. Wallenda, will you talk to these reporters?"

Gunther sighed, "Me?" He shook his head. "I can't talk at all right now. Leave me alone, please."

Today, thirty-some years later, Gunther has given the accident much thought and has come up with his own idea of what happened: "I think Dieter felt pins and needles in his arms from holding the balancing pole so long in one position. He didn't know to curl his wrists so the pole wouldn't get heavy. So he tried throwing it into the air for a second, but he lost control and everything collapsed. When Jana went flying, her chair spiraled by Mario in mid-air and smacked into him; in fact, the doctors found wood splinters in his head."

Whatever was the true cause of the accident, it was a moot point—Karl promised Helen he would never again perform the human pyramid. Although satisfied with his assurance, Helen still refused to watch any of his performances from then on.

That same night Delilah nestled under the Eiderdown quilt in Martha's house—tucked safely and warmly under the covers; Tino was in bed, too. Delilah had played hard all day; she was asleep in minutes. In the middle of the night, the phone a few rooms away screamed so loud it seemed to rend the air. Delilah heard her grandmother cry out. "Oh, no, no, no!" Martha sobbed, her voice cracking. Delilah knew immediately something was wrong with her family. "Oh my, oh dear God," Martha wailed.

Hearing her, Delilah lay perfectly still in bed, afraid to move. She lay there motionless for a long time. Then the nine-year-old raised her head, slowly coming out of her sleep-fog. The grogginess passed, and at last it came to her, first as a smell, that of fear, thick and all-encompassing, then as sounds, the gnashing of teeth, the beating of breasts.

Finally, she forced herself up. She crawled out of bed and went down the hallway. She walked into the room. There she saw it: sheer frenzy, pandemonium—screaming, sobbing, wailing—a form of lunacy, she was sure. Terror spread through her so quickly that she was fearful of becoming sick.

Shaking, she watched the adults—Mutti Martha, Helen,

and Aunt Lottie—fall apart, and she tried to figure things out in her head.

Delilah went to Martha and looked up into her eyes, questioning.

Martha said nothing. Delilah was left to think the worst. Tentatively she asked, her voice high and squeaky and sounding very much like the scared child she was, "My mother?"

"In a few days she'll return."

"I want to see her now."

"When she comes back from Detroit, everything will be explained."

"Is she all right?" pressed the child.

"Later, Delilah. Later everything will be explained to you."

Delilah backed away. She asked no more questions that night, but she never forgot the vision of the three sobbing women.

The next day—because the show had to go on—Gunther, his father Herman, and Mike McGuire climbed the highwire. The second they ran out into the spotlight, spectators hooted and whistled, stomping their feet and clapping uproariously for them. High on the wire, remembering what had happened the night before, they performed headstands on the shoulder bar. The three performers brought down the house. More applause resounded, but the men did not smile in return—they couldn't forget the fall, not even for a second.

Several blocks away, in a hospital bed, Karl watched proudly but tearfully the performance of his brother, nephew, and Mike on television. He wept over their valor and how they were honoring the family code. This was the only time in over forty years that Karl had failed to perform on a scheduled date. He—the mentor—should be with his students. Besides, he thought, what could he do here in a hospital bed? His son was unconscious, Dieter and Dick were dead, and Jana, who no doubt would not want to have anything to do with him again—had been discharged from the hospital earlier in the morning. Lying in bed, he kept rehashing the ordeal, reliving the misery. He decided that whatever surgery he needed, he could do later.

He pressed the call button, and soon a nurse entered his room. "Get me discharged please," he told her while trying to manipulate his bad hip off the bed.

"You can't leave, Mr. Wallenda," she protested.

"I need to be on that wire where I belong." Within hours, he was out of the hospital and back on the wire with Gunther, Herman, and Mike. His temperature registered 102, but he performed all the same, doing the tricks Weitzman once taught him. In mid-wire, he stood on a chair on the shoulder bar and wobbled the chair for effect—the hallmark of an artiste supreme. The audience gasped. In the front row of bleachers in an arena full of spectators sat Jana, watching her relatives climb back on the same wire that had killed her brother.

When Karl descended the rope eight minutes later—his pelvic injury searing hot, his temperature soaring—the audience spontaneously broke into a deafening applause. The maestro walked away, his head bowed, tears flowing. Later Karl told someone that although he had conquered every trick possible on the wire, the one thing he had not mastered was the ability to smile since the deaths. This night he walked out the exit without looking back, and into his dressing room where he was again overcome with emotion. He sobbed again. Gunther tried consoling him by saying, "Uncle Karl, you showed the world that the Wallendas are brave and always the show must go on. We are selling courage."[16]

The next few days passed sluggishly, trance-like, for Delilah, who remained with her grandmother and Lottie. And although she had not been told what had happened, the child surmised that it was an accident. She hung back and watched the women, afraid that something bad might happen to them, too. She listened to them whispering among themselves, watched as they wrung their handerchieves and dabbed their eyes, as though groping their way through darkness.

Delilah struggled through daily activities and prayed that life would return to normal, that everything would go back to how it had been. Finally she was told that the troupe was on its way home and her mother would be there. But because of the tone of voice, Delilah was scared.

The day they came home, she waited at the train station. "It was long, wooden, and one-story, and had arched doors," she says. "I remember seeing Mom get off the train and then we all stood around waiting, which I came to understand was for the caskets."

A long black car arrived and someone told her, "It's a hearse for the coffins."

Still she didn't wholly understand, but as long dark palls were moved into the car and Lottie started howling, Delilah began to put things together. Her young mind discerned that inside those boxes were people she had known and loved. For a long time to come, she would see pictures in her mind of her mother standing with the dead.

After that, things seemed to be happening so fast and in such a haze that Delilah couldn't make sense of the events. A man arrived and stayed near Jenny all the time, taking her arm and ushering her around. Delilah heard her mother tell a friend, "This is Dick's brother." Yet Delilah remained confused. What exactly had happened to Dick?

"Dick was on the wire harnessed to Dieter," Jenny explained later when the child finally got up her nerve and asked about him. "When Dieter fell, he took Uncle Dick with him and they both hit the ground very hard. He died after they got him to the hospital."

Delilah stared at her mother. What about the others? she wondered.

As if reading her child's mind, Jenny added, "And Uncle Mario is very sick. He's still in the hospital."

Sick, how had he gotten sick? Delilah was mystified. She slowly nodded her head as if understanding when she didn't, without voicing her questions.

Later Delilah overheard an argument between her mother and Mutti Helen: "You must go to the funeral home, Jenny; it's your place," step-grandmother Helen ordered.

"I don't want to remember him that way," Jenny replied quietly. "I just want to be left alone at my mother's house."

"That's not right," Helen insisted. "It's your husband and cousin. You must go to the funeral parlor."

Jenny shook her head, paused, then said, "The only thing I must do is buy a plot of land."

Helen said she would sell Jenny a burial site in a cemetery nearby where she and Karl had their own plots and many other Wallendas had been interred.

Jenny thanked her. "Now I can lay my husband to rest."

A black chain fence enclosed the plot.

*   *   *

In the confusing days that followed, Delilah saw the world as if through a veil. Nothing was clear to her. While Jenny battled her own grief, the child remained at home, waiting, struggling with a despair she did not understand. Nor did she understand why there were so many people around— people everywhere, wailing and moaning, coming from places as far as California, Michigan, New Hampshire, Massachusetts. All the commotion increased her concern over her mother, who at one moment seemed angry while the next was crying. For eons, it seemed to Delilah, nothing went back to being ordinary. Instead, things got more confused. Delilah felt more and more frightened. When she was asked if she wanted to go to the funeral of her stepfather and cousin, the child refused. Never did she say good-bye to the man who loved her as his own daughter. Never did she forget or completely forgive herself for not going.

As the days went by, Delilah wondered, Where was Vati? She couldn't really ask anyone. The people going in and out of the house were strangers. The bushels of mail delivered to the adults were secretively taken. Flowers filled the house, and florists dropped off more arrangements daily. With each arrival her mother cried more.

Later, Delilah heard her mother ask Mutti Martha, "Where's Lottie, Mama?"

"She's taken the $10,000 insurance money on Dieter and gone back to Germany with Jana," Martha said, her voice colored by grief. "She's very upset—mad."

"At me?" asked Jenny. "Why me?"

"Because of the accident."

"I can understand her being angry with Papa, but why me?" Jenny was so baffled that she forced herself to think over the past few days to see if she had done anything hurtful to Lottie. Later, she received a note in the mail from Lottie expressing how disturbed she was because Jenny hadn't gone to the funeral parlor or taken good care of Dieter so that he died. Jenny held the letter in her hands a long time, the ache cutting through her the way the wire had sliced through her father.

Jenny comments: "I feel badly that Dieter died, but it wasn't my fault; he made the decision to walk the highwire. I lost my husband, too." She remembered the cards, flowers, letters, and money that mourning fans sent. "All of that went to my father's home, and I never did see them, never did get the money; it happened to Mario, too. And right after the accident my father said, 'Because they didn't cancel our bookings, you'll get your salary for the rest of the year.' Not only did I *not* get the money, but I was charged for the three days I took off for the funeral."

The accident had strained some of those bonds gluing the Wallenda clan together. Loved ones seemed angry and resentful of each other, and animosity deepened. At first everyone attributed it to the grief and tension they were undergoing, but later it seemed more complex.

Karl did not attend the funeral of his son-in-law and nephew. He visited his injured son Mario only infrequently. Instead he continued to work on the road, living by the philosophy that "The dead are gone; the show must go on." Not long after the fall, a reporter approached Karl and asked, "What will you do now, Mr. Wallenda?"

Karl answered in a whisper, "The rest of life is just time to fill in between the acts."

EIGHT

Aftershocks

Change is the only constant in life.

For Delilah, change was the one thing she came to expect in life.

And for her, most changes seemed to create havoc in her world.

The year 1963 came on the heels of the tragic seven-man accident and for the Wallendas proved to be another bad year. It opened with Delilah turning eleven and dealing with her mother's new occupation: running a circus school. Not wanting to return to the wire right away and be reminded of her loss, Jenny opened a school—housed in an old barn—for kids whose parents thought their children were destined to give up books to make big money in show-biz; kids who dreamed of performing on trampolines, the wire, and doing other stunts to impress their peers. Although the idea sounded wonderful to Delilah, like the wire, this business too took Jenny away from her daughter—but at least not far. Still, sometimes Delilah was unhappy at having a working mother. For instance, one morning Delilah woke with a fever and consuming pain in her neck that prevented her from turning her head even a tiny degree.

Jenny placed her hand on Delilah's forehead, felt her neck, and then announced with all the authority of a doctor, "You have the mumps. Stay in bed today."

"But I want to go to the circus school with you," whined Delilah.

Jenny shook her head. "You have to stay home," and then she and Tino walked out the door and headed for the circus school.

Delilah murmured, "It's tough being a kid and sick without Mommy around."

Sometimes, though, Delilah loved her mother's new occupation. One day as Delilah was watching her mother teach, Jenny motioned Delilah to come over to where she was directing her students. "Watch my daughter; she'll show you how to do the stunt."

Feeling pride and accomplishment, Delilah walked toward her.

Jenny told Delilah, "Climb up a little ways and show them."

Delilah looked at her mother, a smile playing at the corner of her lips, and did exactly as her mom dictated. When she got down off the web, she told her mom, "That hurt."

"Then something's wrong," Jenny proclaimed. She thought about the stunt for a while before saying, "I told you wrong."

"Great," mumbled Delilah, trying to act poised in front of all the students.

"Okay," Jenny nodded. "I remember the way to do the trick now. Go back up and do it this way," she said, using her hands to demonstrate.

Obediently Delilah climbed up to the web again. The second she began the stunt, she knew it was right this time and told her mother so.

"Ja," agreed Jenny. "Now let the other kids do it."

Her mother smiled and quickly dismissed her.

Later Jenny, as a way to express her thanks, took Delilah and Tino to a drug store restaurant and ordered the special: a T-bone steak, french fries, and a tossed salad. The three sat on stools, chatting away about this student or that trick and how an act could be improved. Delilah was delighted with her success at the circus school, not only because it was fun and she could demonstrate her ability at different stunts, but also because her mother was not off somewhere performing.

A week later, Delilah and Tino brought their dogs on leashes with them to the circus school.

Shaggie, Delilah's shepherd, barked and yelped. Suddenly, the animal took off running, yanking Delilah so hard that she fell flat on her face, still grasping the leash. Shaggie sprinted about, dragging the child through the high grass. The faster it ran, the harder Delilah laughed, telling her mother afterwards, "It was like being on a carnival ride. I had fun."

For Delilah, her mother's school offered a wonder-world that she quickly adopted as her own.

"In those years, Fridays were my favorite time," she explains.

Around this time, Vati admitted himself to the hospital for surgery on his pelvis and hernia. Unable to relax, Karl required three to four times the amount of sedation normally needed, as well as a straight jacket to control him.[17] Even in an artificial sleep, he relived the fall, seeing clearly that night in Detroit. . . . To him, the Wallendas faltered; each of them had failed—especially he himself, the maestro.

Hours later, when he awoke, he was consumed with determination to restore the family name and honor. He felt empowered to try it one more time, to recreate the human pyramid, to persuade his family to get up on that highwire and once again become the triumphant seven. Perhaps he felt obligated to revive the public's faith in the troupe, or the troupe's faith in itself?

Delilah wondered why he had to persist in his futile death wish. How could Vati even give reforming the pyramid a passing thought? All he had to do was look at his son Mario or gaze into Jenny's eyes and see the pain. What was the point of it anyway? The money? His reputation? Wasn't enough enough?

Only days after he was discharged from the hospital, Karl informed some of the troupe members, "We gonna do the 'seven-man' one more time." He hadn't told his daughter Jenny yet; she had been estranged from him since the accident.

When Karl told his wife that Jenny didn't know, Helen responded, "Well, she doesn't come around much anymore."[18]

"Ja." Karl nodded, and then left to visit his daughter at her circus school. He stood off to the side, watching her perform, pleased with the skill and expertise she had gotten from him. When she took a break, he quickly went up to her, all smiles, and told her how important it was they redo the "seven." "You come back, right?" he asked.

Jenny wondered how he could expect her to return to that moment her husband died.

Karl left satisfied, though he had not extracted any promise from her.

Still, if there was resistance on anyone's part, Karl did not see it. No one tried to persuade him to give up his idea. His word was law.

Although Jenny wasn't happy, the thought of opposing her

father really didn't occur to her. She knew that in the end she would obey his dictates.

Looking back now, Jenny comments, "We never opposed my father. It seemed natural for us to redo the stunt. We were performers, so we just accepted it. And coming from my father, I had no reason to think his judgment was wrong."

Resisting Karl on anything was not only unnatural but unheard of because he had a way of charming people into his way of thinking without even giving them a chance to reconsider.

"My grandfather could convince anyone to do anything he wanted," advises Delilah. "He just had a way about him that wouldn't let you say no. So despite the fact that everyone worried about the pyramid, no one said no to him; they readied themselves for the re-creation." Actually, Jenny had expected all along that he would want to redo it.

One of the driving forces behind Karl's desire to assemble the seven-man was NBC wanting to do a documentary on it for the "DuPont Show of the Week."

Jenny shrugged. "But I am curious about who Papa will get to take Dick's place."

Delilah understood her mother's renewed interest in the wire; after all, it was as natural as her schoolmates' mothers baking cookies for a homeroom party.

However, she knew this also meant her mother would again divide her time between practicing and home duties, with little time and attention left over for Delilah. "When Mom ran the circus school, she seemed less preoccupied and enjoyed being home, but with her returning to that thin wire, I knew her mind would center only on getting back up there. Still, I just accepted that she'd do it, but I can't say that eased my fear that it couldn't happen again—them crumpling forty feet to the ground," says Delilah.

Soon Delilah learned that taking her deceased stepfather's place on the wire was a man named Andy Anderson, who used to do an act—the Roman Ladder—fifty feet in the air. The act was called the Tony Louis Trio. Andy was Dick's good friend. Delilah remembered that he used to come around when Dick had been alive, yet Delilah really didn't know him. For Delilah this new intruder was another cause for fear.

Outside in the yard of the Wallendas' winter quarters in Sarasota, Herman finished attaching a cable snugly to a tree at a practice height of ten feet. Karl called to everyone, "Let's go. Time to start practice."

Suddenly, Jenny appeared before her father. Karl's face lit up and they briefly embraced.[19] They understood the past was behind them and the future lay up on the wire—the one Jenny climbed to practice for the re-creation after closing her circus business to devote time to rehearsing.

When not in school, Delilah watched the troupe rehearse; she understood why everyone walked around as though stepping through a mine field. She too was afraid for them all, but her greatest dread was the possibility of losing her mother . . . permanently. Jenny's flitting in and out of Delilah's life had been distressing, but for her to be gone forever was unthinkable. And Delilah knew it could happen; after all, it had happened to her stepfather and cousin. What was to say that the pyramid wouldn't crumble again . . . this time with her mother on top?

Delilah's thoughts bounced from one ghastly vision to another. Why were the Wallendas in the business of self-destruction? Wasn't it enough that Andy had replaced Dick? How was she to deal with her agonized feelings, especially the hurt she felt over what seemed to be a new favoritism by her father Alberto and her mother toward Tino?

Added to all this was the throbbing pain she felt in her lower left back—the same pain she had experienced when four or five and Jenny had taken her to the doctors, who said that Delilah needed more tests. When Jenny asked what caused her daughter's soreness, the doctors said the child was jealous of her brother and that her resentment mani-fested itself physically. So Jenny had taken Delilah home. After that, when Delilah cried about the ache, Jenny had sternly told her to go to bed, lie down, and rest.

In the next few weeks, Delilah's life seemed to go from bad to worse. Her back pains grew more intense, not only had Andy replaced Dick on the wire but he had entered her mother's life, her parents treated Tino better than her, and the re-creation of the seven-man pyramid unnerved her. She wanted to run into Mutti Martha's arms and cry her tears dry, but Martha was off traveling with her husband J.Y. as part of the Ringling Brothers Circus where she helped out in the concession stand.

Then when Martha returned, in addition to all Delilah's other troubles, the child began noticing disturbing changes in her grandmother. Over the years, Delilah's mother had come to accept Mutti's eccentricities, such as claiming there were odd smells in the house, so Jenny was not too dis-traught by her mother's behavior. However, Delilah feared that Mutti's recent demeanor was something more serious than just "eccentricities"; Martha acted as though someone had attached a key to her back and wound her up too tight.

Jenny reassured Delilah, "My mother's fine; she's proba-bly just going through something." Even though grand-mother's mental state worried her, Delilah pushed the thought to the back of her mind and instead agonized over the 'seven-man.' She watched the new members rehearse every day with Vati. Delilah became aware that he was obsessed with redoing the pyramid. Although most believed Karl got his way by pouring on the charm, some began to whisper of his cruelty and plain meanness, applying pressure to get what he wanted. And lately, noticed Delilah, Vati had seemed to be arguing continually with Mutti Helen, who didn't want him to redo the act.

The old congenial atmosphere had evaporated. An air of dissension descended over the house of Wallenda.

Delilah perceived the troubled atmosphere, and she also noticed during rehearsals for the 'seven,' Andy seemed to be getting closer to her mother Jenny. When Jenny decided to build a cabana—a couple of bedrooms on the back of her trailer—he came around to help. Well, thought Delilah, Andy was just an old friend of Mom's and she needed companionship, and he did take her mind off Dick.

Whenever Andy visited Jenny, he also made time to play football and badminton with Delilah and Tino. In the beginning, he got along fine with the kids and with Jenny, who— at thirty-five—was eight years older than he was. Yet Delilah was wary, hanging back and observing this new thief who was stealing her mother's love.

Then one dark day, as dark clouds thickened and thunder clapped, the troupe assembled once again for practice. They climbed the ladder and stepped onto the high wire, each quiet yet confident, for they were the proud and intrepid Wallendas.

Karl smiled. "Ready?" he called out.

Jenny pulled herself into position as the top-mounter, while Herman slipped his yoke on, making sure he was securely fastened to Karl. Gunther, as usual, carried the tail-end position with aplomb. But while on the outside he modeled as the self-assured performer, inside he was debating about whether to quit the business. He had fallen in love again and felt the troupe had grown callous, seeming to forget about the dangers of the "seven," and he was troubled also over Karl's new protégé—Andy.

Gunther told his uncle, "We ought to split the 'seven' up into two different acts for safety reasons."

"Not to worry, Gunther, everything will be fine. We have to do the pyramid for the DuPont special."

Gunther shook his head. "I don't know, Uncle Karl. I've told you before I'm not crazy about this idea. You remember I have a daughter to raise, and I've already lost Margarita to the circus. I want to marry Sheila and live a life without her worrying about me being on the wire."

Karl slapped his nephew on the back. "It'll be fine, you'll see. This will be our last time doing pyramids. C'mon now, let's do a good job."

Everyone seemed to believe Vati. His old magic had resurfaced. On this day the slug moved slowly but comfortably across the wire. Everything seemed to work. It appeared that the Wallendas would once again reach super heights of prominence and pride.

On the ground, Mario pensively watched from his wheelchair. He would have done anything to be back on the wire. He had even gone as far as asking Herman one night at dinner, "Uncle Herman, can't you rig up something so I can ride the wheelchair across the wire?" Mario conceded that the past would haunt him for the rest of his life. One good thing had come out of the catastrophe: Mario's nurse, Linda, who spent so much time with him in the hospital, had recently become his wife. Mario joked with her, "I only married you because I thought you were rich," and she quickly retorted, "What other reason would I marry you?" and then they laughed. It was a good marriage for Mario. Still, such happiness, although fulfilling, didn't take the place of walking the wire as a Wallenda.

Shaking off his dismal thoughts, Mario smiled encouragement at the seven on the wire. Their moves were the same as a year ago; nothing had changed. He felt pride at their bravado and finesse, seeing, too, out of the corner of his eye that Sheila also stood observing. He knew his cousin Gunther was going to marry her, and he was pleased.

Abruptly his smile faded when he realized the wires were sinking, sliding down the bark of the trees.

Almost at the same moment, the troupe felt a ripple vibrate at their feet on the wire, and visions of loved ones hurtling through the air filled their heads.

"Steady, steady!" Karl called, trying to make his voice sound pacifying.

Mario gripped the wheelchair's arms while Sheila stiffened, holding her breath.

No sooner had Karl turned to locate the problem than the sound of wire twanged in the air and bodies sailed.

They lay sprawled on the ground. Vati went from one to another, calling to each to determine the degree of injuries. His eyes hurriedly spanned the cable and his mind clicked: the cable had slipped inches down the tree. But right now the wire was not his concern—the family was.

Jenny struggled to her feet but couldn't put weight on her ankle. Gunther had lost all of his front teeth. The others were bruised, too.

"I quit!" muttered Gunther through a mouthful of blood and broken enamel.

Karl stood up to him. "You can't quit! We're almost there —the 'seven' redone! We must do it one more time; just once, a final time!"

Gunther shook his head, wiped the blood from his mouth as though brushing this part of his life away, and stalked off, moving into a future that did not include the highwire.

Sheila ran up to him and within seconds had him in the car and on the way to the hospital.

Karl was dismayed; everyone was walking away from the wire. "Tomorrow will be better," he called out to anyone who would listen.

Herman stood on the sidelines, blaming himself since he had overseen the rigging. Wearily Jenny headed for Delilah's school to pick her up.

At dismissal, Delilah spotted her mother coming slowly toward her. Delilah ran to meet her but stopped short when she noticed her mother's stumbling gait and saw the worry in her mother's face. Anxiously Delilah asked, "What happened? Why are you limping?"

Jenny shrugged, looking away from her daughter. "The 'seven' fell in practice. Gunther quit."

Trembling, Delilah lowered her eyes to the ground and sheepishly followed her mother to the car. She said nothing but feelings of fear quickly spread through her. They did not leave her for a long time.

Days later, impervious to fear and unaffected by the fall in practice or any portent, Karl forced his disciples to shape up for their ten-day engagement at Fort Worth, Texas, and for the DuPont special while he hunted for someone to replace Gunther. Many he approached refused, unwilling to risk their lives for a stunt that might once again misfire. But, as usual, Karl used his charm, as if he had magically snapped his fingers, to produce Gunther's replacement: Chico Guzman, Carla's third husband.

Not long afterward, Karl began practice again. The troupe's mood was somber as they mounted the wire. At Fort Worth, Karl worked them hard.

"Papa, can't we quit for now? We've been traveling all day and everyone is tired," pleaded Jenny.

Karl snapped back, "We're going to practice, no matter how tired everyone is. We might not need it, but the replacements do. I'm not going to let it happen again!"[20]

The new seven obeyed. Up forty feet in the air, their heads nearly touching the arena ceiling, the seven performers looked calm, each concentrating on every step their elk-skin-slippered feet made. Jenny held her balancing pole to her lap, waiting for the slug to stop in the middle of the wire, so she could climb her way to a standing position on the shaky chair. It seemed to take forever before the pyramid reached the middle. Jenny braced her feet around the legs of the chair, lifted her rear off the seat, and managed to pull her body to a semi-standing pose, and then in one easy motion, she rose to a full standing position atop the chair. Her heavy balancing pole glued her to the pyramid. She sensed every quiver, heard her own and the others' deep breathing, and could almost feel the sweat rolling down their faces. She reminded herself that she was a pro and could remain in that position for as long as required before having to slowly fold herself back into a sitting pose. Up there, where life and the well-being of others were dependent on her every motion, she closed off irrelevant thoughts and centered her mind only on her calculated movements, her brain forcing each of her muscles and nerves to perform according to her orders.

Standing, Jenny remained on the chair, and then with slow deliberate motions, she pushed the pole away and then brought it back in to start the opposite process—returning to a sitting position. She was rigid but confident, every cell in her brain focused on performing each step, concentrating so much she was not even aware of her surroundings: the empty arena that soon would turn into a packed house, her father and uncle a level below her, the heat enveloping her, sucking up her oxygen.

Suddenly the lights went out! The pyramid was hurled into total darkness, a blackness so thick it was as though the slug was instantly blinded. Automatically Jenny froze. Below her so did everyone else. From a pitch blackness so dense it seemed to be cutting off her breathing, her father bellowed, "Everybody stand still! Don't move!"

One of the members yelled out, "The exit signs! Look at the exit signs!"

The glow behind the cut-out letters was the only illumination in the profound inkiness, but it was enough to hold them bonded to the wire until somehow the house lights popped back on. Then Karl told his troupe, "You see, you are so good, you can even do the pyramid in the dark!"

Despite the rehearsal problems, the seven-man act went flawlessly on opening night in Fort Worth. When the troupe had reached the platform and taken their bows, the audience sang with praise, rising out of their seats in respect and admiration. The performers patted each other on the back, grinning wide and hailing their bystanders as they ran off to their dressing rooms. The seven-man had finally been done again.

The act at Fort Worth became better with each of the seventeen performances.

But at the end, Herman resigned from the troupe at age 62, forty years after he had signed on with his younger brother Karl, who vowed to continue alone if necessary—as the world's best highwire walker.

Delilah relaxed a little when the Texas engagement and all the seven-man re-creations were behind her. Still, she was alert, keeping her eyes glued on Andy, who seemed to have captured Jenny and the Wallenda clan's admiration.

* * *

About the same time as the Fort Worth performances, sometime around March 1963,[21] Yetty, Helen's sister and the wife of Arthur, Karl's brother, prepared to perform on the highpole in the Omaha Shrine Circus. Her billing likened her stunt to angels swaying on clouds—an act requiring the bravery of a sky jumper millions of miles up in the atmosphere. In this performance, Yetty climbed a pole over fifty feet high, where she wobbled back and forth, contorting her body into a backward position to do a headstand. It was a stunt that left audiences gasping, and she was the best in the world at it.

The year before, Yetty's osteopath had told her to give up the highpole, and she had obeyed until she tired of an idle life. So she had returned to the highpole for one more season, and she seemed happy with her decision. Yet others said later that, as determined as she was to continue with her act, she seemed equally sad and weary.

On this night, she climbed the highpole as she had done for almost a quarter-century and performed her breathtaking act without a hitch, looking in fact better than she had in her younger days.

Finally it was time for her closing stunt, in which Yetty bent over very low as though fixing a foot strap, and then skidded into descent. Spectators loved this part of the act because of its thrill and peril, and Yetty loved doing it for them.

The arena grew dark; the spotlight focused on her. Everyone became perfectly silent as Yetty got into position. Suddenly, she tumbled off the pole, struck a guy wire, and plunged to her death.[22] It was almost as if her movements had been choreographed, they were so graceful and yet so fatal.

When word of Yetty's death came to the Wallendas, the family was greatly saddened. The news seemed to darken Karl's troupe's mood once again. Some considered Yetty's death a premonition, but Karl pushed onward.

NINE

Turmoil

In 1964, Jenny did a stint on the wire with her father's troupe that marked her last time performing with him. Later that summer, Delilah joined her mother and performed the Spanish Web for the Tom Pax Circus. But what's most striking, as remembered by Delilah, was her grandparents' behavior during that time.

Vati's mood seemed more upbeat, but Mutti Martha's did not. Instead, Mutti's signs of deep emotional disturbance increased. Delilah had seen Mutti sitting up late at night smoking cigarettes because she was too afraid to go to bed. And she had noticed her grandmother even had a gun.

Her grandmother's mood swings continued to worry Delilah, who had always had a close relationship with her. She tried to tell herself that it was one of those passing stages adults go through; in no time Grandmother would return to her old self.

Delilah explained, "We used to read the Bible together and pray. We did things like a team all the time. She even converted her porch into a playhouse for me and then would make cookies for me to take to the playhouse. And when her husband—J.Y. Henderson, who is like a grandfather to me—would wake up, he would make us huge breakfasts with steak, and he would go about the house singing. Then suddenly it seemed all that changed, or rather that she changed, but I kept holding on to the past."

For it had been around Martha that Delilah had felt as important as Tino. Martha didn't want to be with Tino more than Delilah, unlike her parents. Alberto had demanded that Tino live with him. Jenny maintained that he couldn't have Tino without taking Delilah. In the end, Alberto took neither child. However, his preference was easy to discern. When he visited, he brought Tino a gift, handing it to him right in front of Delilah, who got nothing. At times Delilah thought Tino had done something to make their father love him more, but no matter how hurt she felt, she continued to adore her brother.

Her relationship with her parents, however, had gotten so bad that Delilah thought about running away. The farthest she ran, though, was into the arms of Mutti Martha. Though Martha's moods were often dark, she still had good days, when she would go shopping. During these times, she bought Delilah and Tino heaps of gifts. Martha had enjoyed studying with her two grandchildren, too, especially Delilah, who rejected school because of the incident in the first grade at the water fountain. Delilah offers, "My grandmother never gave up on me when it came to studying, even though I couldn't read after that paddling. I couldn't do well in school at all. But Grandmother would always study with me and spend time helping me get through, telling me I wasn't stupid. She never put me down for not being able to read. Her loving me was unconditional, even when her moods were dark," says Delilah. "She was beautiful, too. At only sixteen years older than my mother, she didn't look old enough to be my grandmother. She had red hair, and she used to wear orange lipstick and orange fingernail polish. Always she smelled good, and she dressed every day as though she were going out someplace special. Even when she wore pants, her nails would be painted, make-up on, and her hair would be fixed. She was just really special. Everybody loved her, and even today people say how much she meant to them."

Delilah's mother, Jenny, adds, "My mother was so special that my father—even when he was married to Helen—always said he never stopped loving her."

And so, as Delilah agonized over the change in her grandmother—the one person who had seemed to love her unconditionally—she also noted with apprehension new signs of transformation in her mother.

At first Andy Anderson's occasional appearances around the house had not aroused Delilah's suspicions. He was an old friend who came over to help out her widowed mother, and he didn't interfere with the family's lifestyle where unwritten and nonverbalized boundaries existed: Jenny was the boss; Tino, next in line, oversaw his little sister; and Delilah listened to both. Many times the trio did fun things together, and they talked about everything without embarrassment or misunderstanding. Still, Jenny remained a force to reckon with. Her sternness derived from her wanting Tino and Delilah—even though worldly circus kids—reared properly with respect toward others. Only a glance by Jenny sent messages to her children. Delilah says, "My mother talks with her eyes, and I've learned to read them well. She somehow knows everything I do."

One day while Jenny was off working in the house somewhere, Delilah looked outside and saw Linda, Mario's wife, walking down the driveway to the mailbox. The youngster banged out the front door and waved, singing, "Hi, Aunt Linda!"

Linda cupped her hand over her eyes to block the sun. "What are you up to?" she yelled back while grabbing her mail and walking to the edge of her lawn towards Delilah.

"Guess what, Aunt Linda . . . ," began Delilah, talking nonstop about something she'd found exciting during the day. Without realizing what she was doing, Delilah had wandered out of the yard and half-way across the street.

Suddenly Jenny burst out the door, across the lawn, and over to Linda's driveway, where Delilah stood talking, animated. "I told you not to go out of the yard!" she yelled, smacking Delilah.

Linda, who felt badly for not restraining her niece, especially knowing how strict her sister-in-law was, tried calming Jenny, but to no avail. When disciplining her children, Jenny concentrated solely on that. Linda offers, "Over the years, I've seen Jenny so adamant about teaching her children right from wrong that she's beat up Tino, who's a good size, and even Ricky."

Mario adds, "I don't mess with her."

One incident in particular dealing with her mother's sternness remains in Delilah's memory: "There were some people staying at my grandmother's winter quarters, which was where our trailer was. These visitors to Vati's place had concessions there, and they had told my mother that we could get some of the toys from their concessions. Well, my mother said, 'No, you may not have any.' But I felt that it must have been okay since these people told us to take something."

The next day when Jenny left to do errands, Delilah skipped down to the concession trailer and checked out all the inventory. Her eyes fell on a hat. She picked it up, examined it, touching its material, slipped it on her head, and studied herself in the mirror. She decided this was what she wanted. So she carried it back to the trailer.

Later, Jenny returned and saw the hat. "Where did you get that?" she asked, looking at Delilah. When the child honestly answered, Jenny ordered, "I made it clear that you weren't supposed to take something that didn't belong to you."

"But, Mama, they said I could have it."

"And I said you couldn't. Return it, pay for it, and apologize for stealing."

Delilah's eyes widened. "But I didn't steal!"

"Do it . . . now."

The child followed her mother's orders without further protest.

Not long after, Jenny had placed Delilah on restriction for some misconduct. The restriction prohibited her from visiting her friends or having them call on her. And after school, Delilah was supposed to go right home . . . no fooling around or chit-chatting with others. But early the next morning, while Delilah dressed for school, Jenny told her, "I want you to get something for me at the corner store after school."

Delilah nodded, got the details, and then headed off for classes on her bike.

Later in the afternoon, two mean-looking girls eyed Delilah as she came out of the store shoving coins into her back pocket.

"Whatcha doin'," one said mockingly, towering over the child, staring her down.

Delilah felt a chill run through her.

The other came up from behind and pushed Delilah off her bike while challenging, "C'mon, girl, let's fight. Hit me so I can beat you up."

"I'm not going to hit you or get into a fight." Delilah got to a standing position and booted out the kick-stand, intending to ride off.

But each time she tried getting on the bicycle seat to ride off, the two tormentors yanked and tugged at her. And each time, Delilah pursed her lips, dusted herself off, threw her leg over the seat, and tried to pedal away.

Later Jenny came looking for her daughter.

Delilah tensed; she was more afraid of her mom then she was of the two girls, especially when she saw Jenny getting out of the car. In front of the bullies, Jenny screamed at Delilah, "You know you're supposed to go straight home and not visit with friends!"

Hearing Jenny's angry voice, the two ruffians exchanged quick glances and high-tailed it out of there. Delilah did the same, jumping on her bike and outracing her mother home.

Jenny's strict disciplinarian attitude asserted itself in other instances: One day when Jenny was talking with a friend, Delilah, listening, caught a small error in the narration. She gently cleared her throat and interjected, "Excuse me, Mama,
but—"

Jenny's hand swung out and stung her daughter's face.

Delilah pulled back, staring at her mother.

Later, her mother told her, "You know why I hit you when you interrupted . . ."

Delilah shook her head, her palm couching her cheek where the whack still hurt.

"Well," begun Jenny apologetically, "You have to remember I was reared the old-fashioned European way, where children are seen and not heard; I guess I forgot I'm in America, so I raise you the same."

Delilah nodded. She knew as severe as Jenny was, she was just as affectionate. She'd stop whatever she was doing to play with her children, and at bed time, she tucked them in and said a German prayer with them. Always she supported and protected them . . . even against her own relatives.

One time, Mario was outside when he spotted his niece and nephew coming out of their house. He grabbed an old bullwhip and went into his sister's yard, where Tino and Delilah were playing, and began teasing them with the switch, laughing all the while. Jenny happened to glance out the window and saw her brother flashing the whip. She stomped out of the house and over to Mario, grabbed the whip, and began to lash him.

So although Delilah didn't like the discipline, this didn't hinder Delilah from loving Mama and Tino. She had no reservations about approaching her mother with her problems, even if they dealt with boyfriends. Jenny responded openly, and the two would talk things out. There existed a give-and-take in their relationship, and Delilah sensed as she grew up that her mother was becoming her friend.

Tino, too, was turning into an ally whom she had learned to trust. He often played with her, especially games like "foot juggling"—one of the many circus tricks he'd invented. One day he called to his sister, "C'mere, Delilah. Let me show you a trick."

Then he lay on his back, stuck his feet into the air, and said, "Sit down."

"Sit? Where?" she asked, looking around.

"On my feet, see, then I'll launch you into a somersault."

She looked at him, shaking her head. *What is he, nuts or something?* But he was her big brother, and he did watch over her. Believing in him, she did as he directed, climbing up on his feet. He hurled her, and off she went, flying through the air in that somersault form Tino promised her. But she landed on her head, wrenching a muscle. She remained on the ground, whimpering while Tino stood over her, his hand to his chin, muttering, "Wonder what went wrong."

Delilah loved her brother's games, but as Delilah matured,

she came to understand that although she was close to her brother, other new things seemed to engross him, including girls. Female strangers approached her, asking, "You're Tino's sister, aren't you? Maybe we ought to become friends."

Still, the threesome—Jenny, Tino, and Delilah—were content, growing together in their love for one another, despite the aftershocks of the Wallenda fall, despite harder times since Dick's death, and despite Jenny's having to leave them for weeks at a time so she could go on the road with Karl.

Two years went by and Delilah began to relax, feeling that no chaotic changes were in sight. And then, Andy's occasional visits turned permanent. He moved in.

Months went by as Delilah tried to adjust to this new living arrangement. One day Jenny called, "Delilah, Tino, come into the living room, so I can talk to you."

Obediently they left their nooks and crannies, folded into chairs, and waited to hear what was on their mother's mind.

"Andy and I are getting married on October seventh," Jenny said, watching for their reactions.

Since her mother and Andy had been living together for about six months, the disclosure was not altogether a surprise. Yet for some reason Delilah hadn't expected it either. "Why?" asked Delilah.

Jenny eyed her daughter for a few seconds before answering, "I'm going to have a baby."

Impetuously, Delilah jumped up and hugged her mother; Tino too hugged and congratulated her.

Over the following months, Delilah noticed that her mother was devoted to Andy, and most of the time he behaved like an adoring husband and good father. But Delilah was becoming more instead of less leery, because occasionally she saw a different side of him, the times his temper flared or he got mean and rough when losing in some game with her and Tino. Still, she had no real problem with him. He generally treated her kindly, and so she accepted him just as she had accepted Dick.

Because Andy was a circus man, too, he fit quickly into the rest of the Wallenda family. Then he convinced Jenny that he and she should go on the road with their own act.

However, their being on the road brought Delilah more turmoil.

"During this period," begins Delilah, "I was again volleyballed between living at home and living with relatives. By the time I got to eighth and ninth grades, I was relegated to taking correspondence courses when I did get the chance to go on the road with my mother. Only once in tenth grade, when I lived with my Uncle Gunther and his wife Sheila, did I go to regular school for any length of time. I never did graduate from high school."

Andy, however, was enthusiastic about being on the road with his and Jenny's own act. He comfortably situated himself in the role of circus businessman, loving husband, and tolerant stepfather. As time went on, Delilah sometimes thought he got too comfortable in the role of father because he seemed to grow bossier, stricter, and even sterner than Jenny.

Not only did Delilah have doubts about Andy, she found it strange to see her mother pregnant and due any day. Yet there was a kind of joyousness about it. Delilah watched her mother and Andy to see how this new baby would affect all their lives.

When Jenny went into labor and had a baby girl, a sense of exhilaration permeated the house. Finally, the moment of their homecoming arrived. On a cool March in 1965, Andy, Jenny, and baby Tammy pulled into the trailer's driveway. Delilah observed their arrival from a window, excitedly.

Delilah ran from the window to the front door to let them in. She could not wait to hold the infant, cuddle her, let her know she had a big sister. "Hi!" she greeted them enthusiastically. "Please let me hold her!" Her arms reached out to clasp the baby.

"No," Andy said reproachfully, "you can't go near the baby. You have a cold. Stay away."

"But . . . but—"

"I said no," repeated Andy.

Delilah backed off, feeling hurt and neglected. Throughout the next days she watched everyone calling on the infant and holding her. Delilah consoled herself: Her banishment was only a temporary setback. Soon she'd be over her sniffles and could snuggle with the baby, making Jenny as proud of her as she was of the new addition.

In a way Delilah was rewarded because soon she was able to hold the baby. However, the baby proved to be more than cuddly—it was downright demanding, hogging her parents' attention, needing things at unreasonable times, and expecting all to move at her every cry and yelp. Often it was Delilah who was required to respond to the infant's needs. Without realizing what was happening, the youngster discovered she had become a built-in sitter and nursemaid.

She comments, "There were times during my teen years when all my friends were going out but I wouldn't be allowed to join them because I had to babysit Tammy. I felt like a maid, and I only got $5.00 a week for all the work I did. I never hated Tammy; in fact, I loved her immensely, but I did hate having to give up my life all the time to take care of her. And I must admit . . . she was spoiled."

Still, the teen harbored no resentment toward her baby sister, and as greatly as she loved Tino, she loved the new addition nearly as much.

However, Delilah became more and more indignant about the scud work to which she was assigned, and she began to experience a sense of rivalry over the devotion and love Jenny heaped on the baby. The old talks she used to have with her mother about boyfriends and growing-up problems no longer took place, not only because Tammy kept everyone on their toes, but also because Jenny concentrated too much on Andy. Delilah felt neglected whenever she saw her mother occupied with Tino or Tammy or Andy and not with her. She felt that now her mother had a new little girl and didn't care about her any more. What was worse was that she knew she shouldn't feel this way, yet she couldn't control her rancor. The more she tried, the more evidence was presented to her that her worst fears might be true and that she was no more than a servant. A disturbing episode hammered home this point:

Tammy was ten months old when Andy walked into the kitchen, where Delilah was cleaning dinner dishes, and told her, "Your mom's not feeling well. Probably the flu, but I'm going to run her down to the doctor."

"Gee, I hope she's all right."

"I'm sure she will be, but I need you to watch Tammy."

Delilah nodded.

"And don't forget your chores," he warned as he escorted Jenny out to the car.

While they were gone, Delilah stayed in the camper's kitchen with Tammy, intending to get the dishes done before they returned. But the toddler wanted to play, and she took Delilah's attention away from her chores. Soon they were rolling on the floor, playing, giggling, tickling each other. The teen forgot all about doing the dishes.

Andy entered the trailer, snarling, "Look at this kitchen! I told you to clean it."

"But I was watching Tammy . . . we were playing—"

"Never mind that! I told you to do your chores," Andy insisted.

Delilah hurried to get the dishes going, but little Tammy didn't understand that playtime was over. So from the floor she kept pulling on Delilah to play, and every time Delilah nudged her to the side, she yanked Delilah all the harder.

"Leave me alone, Tammy," said Delilah, irked with the child and upset that her mother and Andy were treating Delilah so miserably.

Tammy kept tugging on Delilah's slacks and stepped in between the sink and her sister.

"Stop it, Tammy," Delilah said, afraid Andy would yell some more about the dishes not getting done.

Again the tyke whined and stepped in front of Delilah. Delilah picked her up and moved her to the side. The second Tammy's feet touched the floor, she lost her balance and fell.

"Don't ever push her again!" yelled Andy.

"I didn't push her," Delilah protested.

"How dare you do that to my daughter!" screamed Andy, running toward Delilah.

"It was an accident!" Delilah's voice cracked as she began to cry.

Outraged, Andy picked Delilah up and hurled her against a wall.

Panicked, Delilah couldn't move. She saw Andy pick up one of Tammy's toys, and in the next instant he was hitting her with it.

When Jenny did nothing to stop Andy, Delilah felt betrayed by her mother. Tino, however, emerged from some room in the trailer and immediately jumped in between Andy and his sister.

Tino's action defused his stepfather's fury. Andy walked away, leaving Delilah crouched in a corner, crying. Tino lifted her up and hugged her.

For Delilah, her brother was a savior, friend, counselor, and protector all wrapped into one, though he was not always there to rescue her.

And in order to survive, Delilah learned to expect the unexpected.

When she was about thirteen, she and her mother were in the yard talking when up walked one of Jenny's friends, Manfred, who started gabbing with her mother. Delilah hung back, allowing her mind to float. An old song took root in her mind and she started singing, "Make me, make me your baby . . ."

Jenny spun around, reached across Manfred, and back-handed Delilah across the mouth. "I don't ever want to hear you sing that song again!"

Delilah held her sore cheek. "It doesn't mean anything; it's just a song."

"I know what it means—that you want someone to make you pregnant."

At first Delilah was dumfounded; then she tried explaining to Jenny that the song meant a boy wanted some girl to make him her boyfriend.

Jenny stared at Delilah for a long moment, then turned her attention back to Manfred, picking up where she left off in the conversation.

So between Jenny's rigidity and Andy's temper, Delilah felt as though she just wanted to grow up and get away from home, especially since she couldn't stand the constant bickering between her mother and Andy. As time passed, Delilah perceived that many of the problems she and Andy had stemmed from his relationship with her mother. Still Delilah resented his authority, especially when her mother had been the sole disciplinarian all those years, and she deplored how Andy treated her mom.

Delilah said nothing to him about his behavior, but Tino disgustedly rebelled. A running fight between him and Andy began. Delilah got caught in the middle: she wanted harmony in the house and was willing to tolerate Andy's domination, but she also wanted her brother to be happy, chiefly because her loyalties lay with him.

The best periods for Delilah were when she was on the road with her mother and Andy, who had begun to perform their own act, although they also periodically did some "spot dates" for Vati. Delilah liked this because occasionally she got to work with them, and on the road they treated her differently, as if they were glad she was with them.

But as Delilah's fourteenth birthday approached, she yearned to be free of her chores and babysitting. She wanted to be like the other kids she knew, to live a teenager's life. She reassured herself that her time would come. The end of the year was near; maybe with the new one, she'd have a new life.

But the year ended on a worse note than it had begun.

Andy and Jenny accepted an engagement away from home that left Delilah, Tino, and Tammy with Mutti Martha. Helen, who lived next door was alone, too, since Vati was on the road.

As soon as Jenny and Andy left, the children began playing, running around between Martha's and Helen's homes, seeing both grandmothers and getting whatever cookies and treats they could. During one of the times Delilah ran over to see Mutti Martha, she noticed that her grandmother was going on and on about smells in her house—odors like perfume, which she hated, gas, and even rats.

"Gas?" repeated Delilah, who did a quick check around the house. "I don't smell anything."

This, however, didn't stop Martha, who persisted in her grumblings. J.Y., Martha's husband, acted as though Martha's rantings were as normal as stars emerging at night, so Delilah tried to put it out of her mind. However, after lunch, J.Y. and Martha were entertaining a friend when Delilah heard muttering through the walls, as though her grandmother was agitated. Soon the front door shut and Delilah heard "good-bye" and "come back again." She knew the guest was leaving. A few minutes later J.Y. and Mutti Martha began arguing. Delilah listened. J.Y. was yelling: "I don't understand! What's wrong with him? You've known him for a long time." He slammed something down.

Martha answered in a concerned voice, "He scares me."

"Scares you? Everything scares you!"

Finally, the disagreement ended and the two went about their business the rest of the day, although Martha continued to act despondently.

When bedtime came, Delilah kissed her grandmother good night, but Martha showed no expression. Delilah could tell she was still upset about her fight with J.Y.

Shortly, Delilah and Tino went to sleep. In spite of the day's disturbing events, Delilah snoozed soundly.

The next morning broke amid clouds and a light drizzle. Tino and Delilah rose and moved about, getting ready for school. Leaving the bathroom Delilah spotted her grandmother standing immobile in the living room doorway, her face etched with worry.

"Mutti, what's wrong?" she asked, approaching the woman she loved as much as her own mother.

"Mutti?" Delilah repeated, growing more agitated because her grandmother seemed so unresponsive.

Suddenly Martha turned on Delilah: "Don't stand by me. Get out of the house! They're going to kill us! The gas is coming down. Go away! They're going to gas us!" Violently she shoved Delilah away.

Frightened, Delilah looked around for Tino while J.Y. was already in motion.

"Martha?" J.Y.'s voice rose. He turned to Delilah, ordering, "Take the baby over to Helen."

Delilah grabbed Tammy, waking her from her sleep. She covered Tammy's head with a blanket to deflect the rain.

Martha glanced at Delilah, then at the baby. Seeing Tammy's face covered, Martha's body stiffened, her eyes grew wide, and her mouth opened as if to scream.

Delilah gripped Tammy tighter. Never had she seen her grandmother like this. She wanted to run and cry.

Martha stomped over to Delilah, and immediately Delilah backed up. Pointing a shaky finger at the infant, Martha screamed, "Look, they already killed the baby."

Terrified, Delilah changed out of the house and across the yard to Helen's. Tino stayed with J.Y. and Martha, waiting for the doctor.

Shaking, Delilah watched from Helen's window as the paramedics took Mutti away.

Afterward, Delilah learned that Mutti had been admitted to the hospital. Delilah was sure her grandmother would never return to her.

When Jenny returned home, J.Y. told her what had happened.

Jenny remarked, "I can't believe it's a nervous breakdown. What would have caused it? Did she give you any indication?"

"She smelled smells."

"But she's right; I smelled gas as soon as I stepped into the house."

"She's always smelling something," J.Y. snorted.

"Will she be all right?"

"She's on different medications."

"They'll help her, these pills?"

J.Y. looked searchingly at Jenny, then said, "But she doesn't always take them." He paused a minute, coughed, then added, "I took her gun from her."

Jenny's eyes widened, but she said nothing.

Delilah wasn't allowed to see Mutti in the hospital, except for one time when Mutti's was given permission to sit in the lobby where her grandchildren were briefly allowed to visit.

"How are you, Mutti?" Delilah asked, nuzzling up to her favorite person.

Mutti didn't answer but with trembling fingers handed Delilah a belt she had made during her hospital stay.

What frightened Delilah most was how red her grandmother's face looked, and how the woman she had always loved acted like a stranger toward her.

A few weeks later, Martha came home. Soon after, Jenny told Delilah, "J.Y.'s going on the road for a couple of days, so Mutti's coming to stay with us while he's gone."

"Here?" asked Delilah incredulously. "You mean she'll sleep in my room?" She was fearful that her grandmother would behave the way she did the day she broke down.

Her mother patted Delilah's shoulder consolingly.

Besides grappling with Mutti's illness in the days that followed, Delilah had her own never ending flare-ups of pain in her back and side. With their attention on Mutti and performing, no one seemed to understand Delilah was suffering. At the tender age of fourteen, Delilah sometimes wished she could retire from life—which she saw as full-time combat.

TEN

Another Dark Day

A 1966 newspaper article begins:

HIGH WIRE ACT IN THEIR BLOOD

The husband and wife team of Andy Anderson and
Jenny Wallenda perform an act in which Jenny hangs
suspended from a bicycle on the high wire and spins.
The Wallendas are the only act to attempt such a trick
because, according to Andy, "the spinning breaks all the
laws of balance." . . . [Jenny] left the spangled circus
world . . . following the [seven-man] accident. [She]
opened a circus training school and taught eager children and adults aerobatics and trapeze. Then, after 16
months, at the encouragement of her father, she again
went back to the high wire. . . . Miss Wallenda has
been walking the wire for 22 years. [Says Jenny,] "You
get your ankles and wrists open, your back hurts, you
get bruised and you don't think you can go on the next
day, but you know that you have to. You rehearse and
practice."

As time passed, Delilah's expertise in the world of circus was expanding and Delilah had begun getting into her mother and Andy's acts more often. Although performing in any act was a beginning, it was not what she eventually wanted to do. In her mind she dreamt of becoming a highwire walker. Although sometimes it seemed that this dream would never come true, Delilah looked forward—a Wallenda trait.

Her focus was on the new year and the hope that it would bring something better. In January, J.Y. left for Ringling, so Delilah went to Mutti's for dinner. The first thing she noticed was that Mutti seemed more distracted than ever. Mutti still frightened Delilah, who had changed toward her grandmother. "I saw something different in her eyes," says Delilah. "Ever since her breakdown she behaved as though a stranger had overtaken her body and mind. To me, she never seemed to be able to recapture her old self. Such a sadness was reflected in her eyes."

"Everything okay, Mutti?" Delilah asked, grabbing the salt and pepper.

"As best as can be expected," her grandmother answered, and then smiled for the youngster.

"I'm going with Mom and the family to Cincinnati, where they have a booking," Delilah said, trying to make conversation.

"Tell your mother I need to talk to her before she leaves."

"Sure," Delilah answered, anxious to leave.

When Jenny stopped in to see her mother, Martha warned, "I want to tell you something."

"What, Mama?" Jenny asked.

"If someone tells you I killed myself, don't believe it."

Jenny froze with surprise and fear and looked at her mother. She said nothing so as not to further upset her mother, who seemed to oscillate between having good days and bad ones since she had been discharged from the hospital.

Not long after, Jenny's family—Tino, Delilah, Tammy, and Andy—went on the road to Ohio to do their highwire act in a Shrine circus while Martha, who was still acting strangely, and J.Y. went on a stint with Ringling in Washington, D.C.

Vati had slowed down, accepting a full-time directorship with Tom Toy's Shrine Circus, headquartered in St. Louis. To everyone's surprise, he seemed to be standing by his word to Helen that the directorship would serve as a form of semi-retirement.

Delilah was excited about her trip to Cincinnati, but she was worried about Mutti, knowing something was wrong.

On March 23rd, only a few days after Jenny's family had arrived in Ohio, a circus office worker hurried to her trailer.

"What is it?" Jenny anxiously asked as she answered the door.

"There's a long distance call for you and you're to return it right away." The clerk turned and departed.

Jenny looked at Andy. "I don't know . . . ," she began.

"Don't worry," he soothed, "I'll take care of it." He shut the trailer door behind him and went to answer the call.

Jenny waited anxiously. When Andy returned, his face was pale, a mirror of grief and sorrow. Immediately Jenny knew something was terribly wrong. "My mother! My mother! Oh my God, she's dead! She's dead! I know it!"

Andy nodded, walked over to his wife and held her as she collapsed.

"What's wrong?" Delilah nervously called out when she saw her mother so upset.

Andy told her, "While Martha and J.Y. were at Ringling's, J.Y. took the dog for a walk. Returning, he heard a sound like someone shooting one of those carnival air guns. He ran

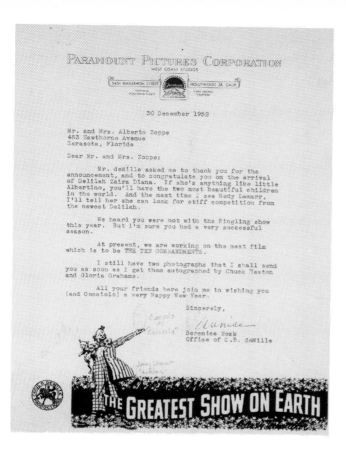

30 December 1952

Mr. and Mrs. Alberto Zoppe
453 Hawthorne Avenue
Sarasota, Florida

Dear Mr. and Mrs. Zoppe:

Mr. deMille asked me to thank you for the announcement, and to congratulate you on the arrival of Delilah Zaira Diana. If she's anything like little Albertino, you'll have the two most beautiful children in the world. And the next time I see Hedy Lamarr, I'll tell her she can look for stiff competition from the newest Delilah.

We heard you were not with the Ringling show this year. But I'm sure you had a very successful season.

At present, we are working on the next film which is to be THE TEN COMMANDMENTS.

I still have two photographs that I shall send you as soon as I get them autographed by Chuck Heston and Gloria Grahame.

All your friends here join me in wishing you (and Cucciolo) a very Happy New Year.

Sincerely,

Berenice Mosk
Office of C.B. deMille

THE GREATEST SHOW ON EARTH

A letter of congratulations from Cecil B. deMille's office on the birth of Delilah Wallenda.

Young Martha Wallenda, Karl's first wife, in 1934.

Karl and
Delilah
Wallenda,
1970.

Delilah performs "the chair pyramid" with Louis Murrillo and Tino
Wallenda, 1971.

Delilah performs "the revolve" with Tino and Louis.

Louis Murrillo, Delilah, Karl, and Tino in Clarksburg, West Virginia, in the early 1970s.

Karl inducts a new member into the family, Lijana, as Delilah looks on, July 1977.

Terry Troffer and Delilah, 1978.

Photo: Dennis Yeandle

A new generation of Wallendas perform "the seven-man pyramid" for the 1977 film *The Great Wallendas: (clockwise from top)* Delilah, Louis Murrillo, Terry, David Klukow, Farrell Hettig, Tino, and Ricky.

At Karl's Sarasota home during the filming of *The Great Wallendas: (top row)* David Klukow, Louis Murrillo, Lloyd Bridges, Karl, Terry, Farrell Hettig; *(bottom row)* Ricky, Delilah, Rietta, Tino.

Delilah prepares the chair pyramid with Terry *(front)* and David Klukow, 1980.

Terry and Delilah under the big top, 1982.

Photo: Tom Spain, Saturday Post Courier

Delilah performs her first skywalk between two buildings at the 1986 Spoleto Festival in Charleston, South Carolina.

Delilah and Terry in Concord, New Hampshire, in 1984.

Photo: Ken Williams, Concord Monitor

Four generations of wire-walking women: *(from left)* Lijana, Jenny, Helen, and Delilah.

Delilah and Terry.

up the path to the train car, and inside he found Martha lying in a pool of blood."

Delilah went white.

Andy added, "Some think it's suicide."

Jenny left Delilah to tend to Tammy in Ohio and returned home with Tino.

Offers Delilah, "When I realized that Grandmother Martha had died I cried and cried. Then I tried to block it all out and went back to behaving like I usually do when faced with problems—just withdraw, go silent."

As the time for the funeral drew near, Delilah found that she couldn't block out Mutti's death the way she had done with others. She grew aloof and moped about. Her mother told her, "Delilah, you should go to your grandmother's funeral."

"No," she responded. So as with her stepfather, Delilah never bid a final good-bye to the woman who countless times served as her mother, friend, and confidant.

In the following weeks, Delilah again worked at cloaking the pain, although she was largely unsuccessful at it. She tried hard to concentrate on things around her—things that she could control—but every time she saw J.Y. getting on with his life, thoughts of Martha resurfaced. Delilah says, "Maybe if J.Y. hadn't come around so much, I could have gotten over Martha, but it seemed as though he was at the house every second." To top things off, he began to show signs of favoring Tino, just as her father did. Delilah said to Jenny, "He always liked boys better than girls; he even admitted that."

Within weeks, though, J.Y.'s attention was diverted by another woman whom he began to date. A short while later he married her. His new wife refused to let Delilah into the house and disliked the family so much that she literally built a wall between Martha's and Karl's properties. Jenny dubbed the structure "the Berlin Wall."

Equally discouraging for Delilah was how sad her brother sometimes looked. She thought it stemmed from his relationship with Andy. The fear that Tino would leave her and strike out on his own edged its way into Delilah's mind. Nearly every day Tino and Andy argued about something— about everything. Delilah's own relationship with Andy had hit a plateau. Both tried to stay out of one another's way. In a distracted state, Delilah went through her days performing with her mother and Andy in some acts, having to take correspondence courses, or staying with relatives. She prayed that Tino would not go away.

However, within months, her mother and Tino had their worst shouting match. "I thought you were only doing the salute on the wire!" Jenny yelled at her son. "I didn't know you were doing more dangerous stunts!"

"I'm sixteen years old, and I've been on the wire all my life," Tino retorted.

"I don't think you're ready for anything else."

"I'm old enough to make my own decisions!"

"Oh, and you think you're old enough to go with Vati to Germany to work?"

"Yeah," Tino snorted and walked away.

"You're only sixteen. What do you know?" snapped Jenny, who felt miserably about her son wanting to leave. She cried for the next few days heartbrokenly.

"Tino," Delilah whispered to him. "Mama's really hurt. She cries all the time because of the fight you had."

Tino clenched his jaw but said nothing.

Then Delilah caught her mother alone and said, "You know, Mama, Tino feels really bad about the fight he had with you. I think he'd like to make up."

Jenny thought for a moment, then nodded. "Ja."

So son and mother came together but not for long.

"The finishing blow," starts Delilah, "came when my mother and Tino had an argument over his doing pyramids on the wire for Vati. My mother thought he was only doing the salute, and she was upset when she learned otherwise because she didn't think he was ready for anything more. Besides, he was going to Germany with Vati to work. I told Tino that Mom was constantly crying about the fight, and then I told Mom that Tino felt real bad. And so they made up, but Tino went to Germany anyway, where he worked with Vati, Aunt Carla, her husband Chico, and her son Ricky, who started assisting on the wire."

The departure of Tino, Delilah's ally, friend, and protector, seemed more than she could handle, especially with everything else going wrong in her life. Now she had no one to defend her, no one to confide in, no one to share her worst fears and promised dreams. She wanted to weep over his absence and yet she wanted to celebrate his freedom. A part of her understood his need but another part resented it. After all, he had left her to fend for herself. Why couldn't Tino have taken her with him? Feeling rejected, Delilah's withdrawal intensified to the point where she not only continued avoiding Andy but seldom exchanged words with her mother.

About this time, Tammy was at the age of exploration, and she was primarily inquisitive about her big sister's life. One day, Delilah was in her bedroom when little Tammy came toddling in to see what was up. She waddled around on the carpet, looking up at Delilah, touching this and that and wanting attention.

Delilah, who was sprawled across the bed reading, occasionally glanced at her sister. Suddenly there came a loud, pitiful whelp. Delilah jumped up, ran to Tammy, and picked her up, attempting to determine the problem. Delilah carefully examined Tammy and then she saw it—a shiny silver sewing needle jammed deep into the child's heel.

Delilah called out for her mother and Andy, who rushed the screaming tot to the hospital. Tammy underwent surgery to remove the needle. Jenny remained by her baby's side. And again Delilah felt guilty for the incident.

While sitting at Tammy's hospital bed, Jenny said to Andy, "I have to decide: should I go with you to do the highwire act we're under contract for in Omaha, or should I stay with Tammy?" This was a serious dilemma for her: the family needed the money badly, the act—the Jenny Wallenda Duo— centered around her, and to have to cancel it now would be damaging to business. However, her child was hurt. Jenny's mind went back and forth. Minutes later, she decided: "I'm going to stay with Tammy, so I guess we'll have to cancel."

"We can't do that," Andy said. "Hey! What about Delilah! She can substitute for you; I know she can do it."

"No, no, no," Jenny protested. "Delilah has never walked the highwire; she's only practiced at ten feet."

"Still, she can do it," Andy claimed. "I have faith in her. Let her perform with me for the first two or three days, and by then you'll be back," he urged. "I can make it look good. The first day she'll only do the comedy routine on the plat- form. The next day she can walk on the wire and do the salute."

Finally Jenny acquiesced, and her husband and daughter were off for Nebraska.

Delilah's most desired dream, her first day as a profes- sional wirewalker, materialized. At the performance, she was so nervous that she constantly checked her costume. The curtains finally went up and she climbed the ladder to the platform.

Delilah says: "I didn't actually walk the wire when I re- placed my mother, but I did climb the ladder and stand on

134

the platform. Andy improvised so that the act looked complete; what my part was, was to slap him during the comedy routine. I guess my relationship with him ran hot and cold. But doing that small bit on the wire platform just confirmed my desire to be a performer like all the generations before me," she says. "I really wanted to do the highwire, but somehow I felt wouldn't be good enough, so I started practicing on the flying trapeze first. At last I was a performer." All day she felt elated.

But soon her balloon burst. The circus boss told Andy, "Your daughter looks too young to work; I don't want her up there anymore."

Delilah's heart was broken. She felt like a failure. She bemoaned her fate to Andy, "How can I help it that I look younger than my age?"

"You can't," he said. "I understand. Don't worry about it. . . . I'll figure something out until your mother comes. You tried, and that's all that counts."

In times like these, when Andy was very nice to her, Delilah didn't know how to react to him.

A day didn't go by that Delilah didn't want to stay under piles of bed covers. Omaha felt like a freezer.

"What's the matter with you?" Andy asked on seeing her shiver.

"It's frigid up here, paralyzing me."

He laughed. "Here, let me rub your hands and feet to warm you." Delilah was grateful for Andy's kindness.

Later in the year, however, another incident reminded her to continue to be wary of her stepfather. On this day, as usual, Delilah's mother got her 22-cup silver coffee maker going—something she did with regularity since so many Wallendas, other relatives, and friends visited daily. Jenny set the urn on the dining room table where it started bubbling and chugging, filling the home with the fresh aroma of recently ground coffee beans. Her mind elsewhere, Delilah stood nearby watching the pot steam and perk, smoldering away.

Looking for her big sister, little Tammy snuck into the dining room where Delilah was, with the intention of jumping out and yelling, "Boo!" Stealthily the child entered the room, trying to get close enough to her sister to scare her. As she tip-toed across the floor, then leapt into the air, she tripped on the electric cord and pulled down the huge steaming pot.

"Delilah! Delilah!" screamed Tammy. "Please! Help me, help me!"

Terrified, Delilah was frozen, listening to the tyke screech in agony, her baby-soft skin seared and blistering.

Immediately Andy appeared, grabbed his daughter and rushed her to the sink, wetting her down with cold water. Seconds later, he had Tammy in the car, flying to the hospital where she was held for two weeks. Although Andy did not verbally blame Delilah, she herself did. She could neither look in the mirror nor into Andy's eyes, knowing what he must have thouht. Their relationship further deteriorated. After that, for the slightest infraction of his rules Andy would put her on restriction for weeks or months at a time, prohibiting her from going out with friends, except for one night a week, providing he and Jenny weren't going somewhere.

In the next months, as Jenny watched him with Delilah, she seemed to notice for the first time his unfairness. A thick tension developed between Jenny and Andy, which made him turn against Delilah even more. Delilah was bothered most by the way Andy see-sawed between master-monster and all-around good guy. She understood that he had an honorable side to him, but it seemed, she says, "he was usually angrier than nice because of this terribly violent part inside him. But when he wanted to be virtuous, he could sweet-talk anyone." Delilah had seen both sides. Still, she was so needy that she was vulnerable to his candied words. She wanted so much to believe him, but when his actions contradicted his words so many times, she stopped. But then he turned right around and did something nice, such as the time when Delilah crusaded for a car.

"How much money do you have to buy a car?" Andy asked.

She told him, "Not enough."

"I'll give you my Fiat; it's not in that great shape, but . . ."

"Oh, thank you!" she squealed with excitement.

"But look," he said. "You can drive it around the property, but never on the street because it's not safe."

Delilah took her car for a spin around the property every day until she felt confident enough to drive in traffic. Then, she commented to her mother and Andy, "I'm ready to drive on the road now."

"But I told you not to take the Fiat out; I'd worry." Andy's brow narrowed.

"What can I do?" Delilah asked, knowing she didn't have enough cash for a better car.

"I'll take care of it," he promised. A few days later he sold the foreign clunker and called Delilah over. "Here, take this money and use it as a down payment on a better car."

The $300 was enough for down payment on a car. She was indebted to Andy for making it possible.

In 1969, Andy and Jenny advised Delilah, "We're embarking on a new business."

Delilah's mouth dropped open. Did this mean they were giving up the wire?

"We're going to buy a funhouse," said Jenny.

"Yes, it can do well for us. And we expect you to work there," Andy said.

"Me? In a funhouse?" She looked at both of them. "But I want to walk the highwire like Vati."

"You'll still work," declared Andy. "Only you'll be selling tickets."

Delilah felt shattered. She realized that the door to walking the wire wasn't going to be opened by Andy or her mother; she had to find another way to get into the circus business.

As crushed as Delilah was, Vati, too, was experiencing disillusionment. He was tired of working on the ground; he wanted to get back to full-time wire walking. Delilah was aware that rumors were circulating about her grandfather and of such newspaper headlines as "Wallenda Can't Quit Wire." She knew they were true. "Vati seemed so restless during that period," she explains. "I never believed he'd be happy slowing down his activities, as he'd promised his wife Helen, and I couldn't see him in any administrative position, especially as some circus director. He was born to be a performer, and no amount of money or cajoling or threatening could make him retire, at least not happily."

He had always said that the one stunt he would love to do was walk over Niagara Falls. Now he began speaking of it again, but Delilah felt this was a fantasy since the state of New York had a net law, which Vati wouldn't accept. But knowing her grandfather, Delilah was sure he'd come up with something equally spectacular.

Sure enough, he did. While producing the New Orleans Shrine Circus, an insane idea hatched in Karl's mind—with prompting from the world who wanted to see him back on the highwire.

During an intermission in the show, a young woman

asked him if he'd ever thought of walking Tallulah Gorge in Georgia.

Later Peggy Cliffs, the woman's sister, according to Ron Morris's book *Karl Wallenda*, called Karl and arranged a $10,000 fee for Karl's journey across the 750-foot-deep, boulder-strewn chasm without a net. "Karl stipulated the cable be rigged to his brother Herman's satisfaction. It cost a total of $60,000. . . . Peggy assembled a team of structural and landscape engineers, plus workmen, who labored 14 hours a day for three weeks to get the aerial highway erected."[23]

At the gorge on the sunny morning of July 18th, twenty mounted police, other law enforcers, and rescue and engineering teams were on duty. Forty-five shuttle buses provided spectators a ride up and down the gorge, and hundreds of boy scouts combed the area for problems and picked up litter.

Karl's cable was twice as thick as he was used to, but having walked the wire for fifty years, he was sure he could handle it. His initial problem, though, was stringing the wire across the gorge. The riggers tried shooting three harpoons with the cable attached across the gorge to the other side, but all three got lost in the forest below. They kept trying to string the wire by different means until bulldozers made way for the rigging. A computer helped plan the maze of guy wires.

Karl said, "I walk the gorge because I want a challenge. I've done everything else already that's sensational. I don't know what else to do."[24]

The recklessness Karl displayed from this point on caused an understudy to comment, "Karl got harder to hold in a pyramid because he wasn't as smooth as he used to be; I had to tell him I didn't feel safe carrying him anymore on a bicycle."

That Karl was tackling the gorge came as no surprise to his family. After all, he had been taught by Weitzman over fifty years earlier that the only way to please a crowd, and to get work, was to progress to ever more dangerous feats. But many outsiders began to feel that Vati did these dire stunts as a means of committing suicide—a way to pay for the tragedy of the seven-man pyramid.

All the Wallendas were there, except for Carla and her children. Jenny, who came in from Seaside Heights, New Jersey, where her funhouse was, went up to her father with little Tammy in her arms. "Be careful, Papa," she said, hugging him.

"I'm always careful, Jenny," he laughed.

Strolling about was Tino, who walked a short way on the wire as though testing it for his grandfather. The crowds, who had begun assembling the night before, pushed inward. Parades down the streets heralded Karl's attempt. Directly before he stepped on the wire, Karl walked over to where medics awaited him to check his vital signs, especially his heart rate. Another check would be done following his walk. Stepping toward the medics Karl tripped, caught himself with one hand on the ground, and then smiled. Surely this must be a good sign? Or perhaps a bad one.

"Are you worried about the wind up there, Mr. Wallenda?" asked one newscaster.

Karl shook his head. "It doesn't seem so bad. The wind never bothers me . . ."

Of the two poles made for this stunt, Karl chose at the last minute the lighter one, at 45 pounds. From the platform, he took his first step on the wire, and began downhill on the cable for the first several minutes. Karl said into the microphone, "My God is with me. I believe everything will be all right. I know how the Deity feels [up here]."

Half-way through the walk, Karl commented about the

severity of the wind—a wind that seemed to worsen with each step he took. At mid-wire, he did a handstand and then began his ascent up the wire toward the end where the cat-walk awaited him:

> Then he raised his body upside down and stiffened his sore legs as straight as ramrods. He semaphored with his feet, to sell the act, and a roar of appreciation rose from the both edges of the canyon. Below the wind howled. With closed eyes, his lips moved in silent prayer. "Thank you Lord. Thank you for keeping me alive."[25]

He was breathing loudly and heavily. The microphone picked up the labored sounds, but dauntlessly he kept going until the end came into view. Huge crowed were cheering him on. "Helen, are you there? I'm coming," he called out. "My hands and arms are getting tired." Almost sixteen minutes had passed and the platform at the opposite side was at last in sight. Karl commented. "That catwalk . . . the hardest thing to catch." He was more worried about stepping from the steel to the wooden platform than he was about the wind jostling him.

All the while, British executives were filming the affair for the BBC. They dubbed it "A Walk in the Sun." At the end of the wire, Karl stepped on the catwalk and then dropped to the solid ground, basking in the accolades. Seventeen minutes later he was, at last, in Helen's and Jenny's arms. Then he collected his $10,000 and was off to find something even more exciting.

Years later, in a magazine article, Karl admitted, "I tell you the truth, the only time I was ever really frightened was at Tallulah Gorge in Georgia."[26]

To this day, Delilah remembered the clamor over her

grandfather's awesome enterprise. She was as wary of his performing this stunt as everyone else but most of all she wanted to be there with him, watching him as the others did. She wanted to hug him when he came off the wire. However, she had been told she had to stay in Seaside Heights with Andy to work the funhouse.

"My mother and Tammy got to fly to Tallulah to be with Grandfather, but I wasn't allowed to go. I had to stay and run the funhouse. I learned from Andy, who was listening to the radio, that Vati made it safely across the gorge. I just looked at Andy and nodded, then went back to selling tickets," says Delilah.

After the walk, the world again rejoiced in Karl's accomplishments. His success gave his family the feeling that he was invulnerable—a false security.

"I guess we all believed that nothing could hurt him," offers Delilah. "I wanted to be just like him, but I knew I had a long way to go and that maybe I would never become the legend he was. Most important to me was to be able to perform. I didn't even think of asking Vati to take me on at this point, because he had so many people working for him—all those he had trained. My goal, of course, was to follow him, to be able to perform; but at seventeen, it all seemed to me to be nothing more than a dream. Still, Vati gave me the incentive. It was after him that I modeled my life, and it was in his footsteps I followed." Vati told Delilah, "One day you too will do skywalks."

There was nothing in the world Delilah wanted more.

For the next few years Jenny and Andy ran their funhouse when not working the highwire during the spring. Delilah, the designated ticket seller, worked each year until September, when the funhouse would close and she would return to school. At this point in her life, she felt ready to begin making her dream of walking the wire come true. Her mother must have been thinking along the same lines, because one day Jenny said out of nowhere, "You're leaving, aren't you?"

Shocked, Delilah nodded. "I need to learn how to walk the wire like Vati."

"Where will you go? How will you live?"

Delilah shrugged.

"And school?"

"I want to walk the wire."

Jenny said nothing more but went to Vati. Soon, thanks to her mother's efforts, Delilah found herself on the road with Vati and Tino. Tino had been working in the troupe since he had left home; he welcomed her with open arms.

"But the most important thing about this time is that I officially joined Karl's act," says Delilah, who remembers her first time with Vati with absolute clarity: "The act before us was on. We were waiting in the wings, watching them perform a balancing perch act. There was a man who held a pole, and people climbed up on the pole and did tricks on it as he balanced it. But suddenly something went wrong and all four people fell—they were hurt. An ambulance came and got them. But as professionals we had to keep going, so as the paramedics took them out on stretchers, we were going on. I remember that the accident hit me very hard, standing there and watching the ambulance come to take them away. It was really scary to see them crumple to the ground. There was blood everywhere in the ring."

Looking at Delilah, Vati asked, "You okay?"

Hesitantly she nodded. "We follow them?"

"Ja. As professionals we have to keep going," he said as the paramedics took the injured out on stretchers. "Let's go," he added breaking into a run, his right arm out in salutation. The troupe headed for the spotlight. Delilah followed.

However, the accident had unnerved her. Through her mind flashed pictures of the four performing and looking as though they were doing well—then instantaneously and without warning, crumpling to the ground. *What a way to start a career*, she thought, trembling all over.

The next day one of the troupe members told her, "One of the hardest things to do is work right after seeing another aerial act fall, but as professionals we perform, no matter how devastating something is. Always remember that." She nodded. *A professional*, she thought. She so badly wanted to become that.

From then on she practiced all the time on the wire, doing the back revolve—a trick on the shoulder bar on the wire—as well as sitting on a chair on top of the pyramid. Vati often watched her to see if she was doing well, but she was the one who, of her own volition, climbed the wire every free second to go over and over each stunt, aiming for perfection.

"You want to help me, Vati?" she asked him once.

"Bah, why should I teach you on the wire? You'll just get married and leave me."

"Never, Vati, never." Because he was still dubious and she wanted to impress him with her commitment, she practiced by herself or with Tino after their grandfather finished.

Other days, Karl would suggest, "You know, Delilah, it would be good if you tried . . ." this or that stunt, and immediately she would begin practicing it.

Things seemed to be going very well. At eighteen Delilah was finally on her way to a new life, a future she had dreamed about for years—one that focused on her dream of becoming one of Karl Wallenda's troupe. The dream was finally becoming a reality. And like him, no matter what obstacles lay before her, no matter what sadness swooped down upon her, she would work diligently toward fulfilling the goal of being a great wirewalker.

However, in a discordant note, 1970 ended with a sad occurrence: Helen's mother, Delilah's step-great-grand-mother, died.

This time Jenny told her daughter, "Delilah, you need to go to this funeral so that you can deal with death, to understand how real and final it is. If you can go on the road with Vati, you can go to a funeral home and look death in the eyes."

Delilah obeyed.

"But," says Delilah, "seeing Helen's mother in the coffin made me think of Martha. When I got home, I cried and cried. It all hit me then, what death was and how it had taken so many of my loved ones and how it forever dangled above everyone's head, threatening their existence."

ELEVEN

A Dream Come True

During the next year Delilah focused on learning the ropes from her grandfather and brother. With their guidance, she began mastering the balancing pole on the highwire and many tricks. She wondered why she hadn't made this move sooner, why she had even bothered to stick it out at home so long. When not working the wire, she acquired extra jobs to help make her $68.00-a-month car payment. Having never had this kind of responsibility before, she relished it now, and even found it "endurable" to return home when not on the road, since her mother and Andy seemed to be trying to respect her new-found maturity. Right after she made her November payment, she decided to go home and called Jenny.

"Get home by three; I want help with Thanksgiving dinner," said Jenny, who couldn't help still asserting her motherly role.

"Mother," Delilah protested. "I'm a big girl now and don't need a curfew."

"Who cares how big you are? You're still my daughter and I want you home."

Delilah was an hour late getting home. Jenny stood at the door waiting for her. "You disobeyed me, defied me. Give me your car keys. . . . No car for a whole week."

Flabbergasted, Delilah handed her the keys, mumbling, "Okay."   Still, nothing bothered her for long, because she was ecstatic that she was finally on the road with Vati and Tino. If she could manage to stay awake every minute in every hour of the day, she believed she would still not experience all of life and its wonders. To the eighteen-year-old, every day had become a marvelous, exciting experience.

Her dread was that all this was too good to be true. She feared that soon everything would come to a screeching halt and God would punish her for enjoying herself so much.

God . . . often she found herself thinking about Him, wondering if Martha was with him. She wondered how she could find Him and went on searching.

On the road, she lived with Tino in a camper. He told her about the wire and taught her the basics: to never, ever let go of the balancing pole, to catch the cable if she was falling, that not landing right was what killed. In practices, both Tino and Vati pounded into her head to concentrate on taking each step and always to check the guy wire before she started walking across the wire.

"Never, ever start out on that wire without first personally checking the rigging," Karl warned her over and over.

Each time he said it Delilah nodded, not realizing those very same words would one day come back to haunt him.

Between practices, Delilah took a little time off to play. One day she decided to visit friends in Erie while Tino was nearby seeing a girl named Olinka Bertini. Her Erie friend had horseback riding stables, and Delilah pitched in helping with the customers.

Delilah mounted a good-sized stallion and gently booted it with her shoes to get it moving. "Follow me," she told the customer behind her. "This is the path you go down." Just as she turned, her horse suddenly broke into a gallop, Delilah bouncing around on its back. She held on tightly, but within seconds, she flew off the horse and hit the ground hard. The horse ran over her in his frenzy.

"Are you all right?" called out the customer. But before she could answer, he was down the path with his mare.

Moaning, Delilah struggled to her feet, feeling pain tear at her ankle. It throbbed so savagely that tears rolled down her cheeks. Not wanting to alert her friend, Delilah climbed back on her horse as if nothing had happened.

"Everything okay?" her friend called to her, as Delilah reined up at the stable.

Delilah labored to smile at her.

However, her expert equestrian friend recognized that something was wrong. "You're hurt, aren't you? My horse threw you, didn't it?"

Delilah confessed that she was in great pain and could hardly walk on her ankle, which was rapidly swelling.

"I'll get Mom," said the friend.

"No, no, please don't," Delilah pleaded. "I'm so embarrassed."

Her girlfriend made a clucking noise but conceded.

Two days later, Delilah took a bus to Utica, New York, where she was supposed to meet Tino at the bus station. When she arrived, he was not there; she had to limp her way to Olinka's house.

Seeing her limp, Tino pointed to her ankle.

"What happened to it?" her brother asked.

"I fell off a horse, and I was more worried about my ego than my injury. I paid for it, though."

"I hope you don't fall off wire the way you do horses," Tino teased.

Weeks passed before her foot went back to normal.

Finally Delilah was able to get back to work, rehearsing on the wire so that she would be prepared for her upcoming performance. The date arrived before she realized it. The first routine she did was the "salute": she made her entrance, climbed up to the wire, lifted one leg, and hailed the audience, much like a sailor saluting his admiral. This went easily for her since she had done it before on the lowwire. However, she was not used to the quick turnaround in tearing down and setting up. Before she knew it, she, Tino, and Vati were on their way to a park for the summer. There Delilah kept practicing day and night; seeing her diligence, Vati forgot his admonition that she would run off and marry.

He began spending time teaching her.

A few months later Delilah, Tino, Louie Murillo, and Karl were performing for a Florida housing development. From there, they did several "spot dates": Providence, Rhode Island, Old Forge, New York, Davenport, Iowa, St. Paul, Minnesota, Omaha, Nebraska, Fargo, North Dakota, Grand Forks, Michigan, Sioux Falls, Iowa.

At the Enchanted Forest in Old Forge, New York, Delilah started practicing the chair trick two feet off the ground. Tino asked, "Want me to help?" He set the chair on the wire and stood on the ground, with his hands straddling the chair to catch his sister if she started to fall.

Later Delilah got enough courage up to practice the trick at thirty feet. When Karl saw his granddaughter up on the wire, he stood underneath, watching her, his face full of pride, smiling. "Good, good," he said.

"We practice for months," advises Delilah, "and sometimes even for years before we go up really high. We begin at two feet off the ground, then go to ten feet, and finally—when we're confident with the trick—we go to thirty feet or higher. Sometimes a trick that we do at lower heights never makes it to the highwire because it just doesn't work up there."

Delilah doesn't think her family—especially her mother—really wanted her on the wire because of its dangers. Yet, she devotedly stuck to it and determinedly forged ahead and bullied her way into the family wire world, practicing such ominous stunts as the "back revolve."

With Karl and the others at Enchanted Forest was Delilah's cousin Ricky. "Enrico wasn't there all the time; just occasionally. And when he was, he sometimes got fired by Vati," clarifies Delilah.

Business that summer was poor and Vati's temper, as well as everyone else's, suffered.

One evening Tino said to his sister, "Let's take a drive up to Utica's ice rink so I can practice skating."

Knowing Tino was working on a comedy routine on ice, she agreed, but added, "Utica's 80 miles away."

As they drove, Tino asked, "Why do you think the crowds are staying away from the shows when this year's program is the best ever produced?"

She shrugged. "It's had lots of publicity, so it should be packed. Maybe it's the gas crunch."

Tino turned and looked at her. "Rumor has it that we might not get paid."

The rumor proved to be correct. Karl called his troupe together and said, "Look, no one's coming to any of these circus shows. It's only gonna get worse." And it did get worse—the show folded. Delilah and the others got some compensation, but Karl didn't take any of the money due to him, wanting to make sure his underlings were reimbursed first. To make sure there was more work, he soon left to pick up another job in West Virginia for the Osiris Shrine Circus. The troupe followed him.

The performance in West Virginia was on a Friday night. Karl was preparing to take his first step on the wire. "Ready?" he asked his 29-year-old son-in-law Chico Guzman, Carla's third husband. Karl was up 30 feet on the platform.

Chico nodded, hanging onto Vati's balancing pole, which he would hand him. Suddenly, Karl detected flashes of colorful sparks. It took him seconds to realize that his son-in-law had brushed against an electric clamp and had been knocked onto a hot wire. Chico was instantly electrocuted, and the electrical force flung Chico 50 feet away from the wire to the ground. Ohio Valley General Hospital pronounced him dead.

Another Wallenda member was gone. At home, word of Chico's death came; this accident further traumatized Delilah. It rammed home once again the fact that in the business there were no guarantees, no promises of safety, security, or continued life.

In the days that followed, Delilah saw how crushed her Aunt Carla was by her husband's death. What was even more visible was the danger in the nature of the work, but Wallendas are not cowards—six generations had already proven that, and Delilah was determined not to be the first to back down. She continued working the wire, more intent than ever to be as good as her relatives before her.

The performers did a number of other bookings before ending their tour in Detroit. At each place, Delilah performed 40 feet up in the air, and then descended the rope hand-over-hand when the act was over and took her bows. Performers don't go down the same way they go up: instead of using the ladder, they slide down a rope. This routine was something she had learned from watching her grandfather and mother all those years, and it was now second nature to her.

Still, things could happen.

During their final stop in Detroit, Vati and his troupe raised their arms as usual to bid farewell to the audience and then stood poised on the platform, ready to descend.

"That day in Detroit, when we were performing with the ice circus, Vati came down the rope with his legs piked, as usual. For some reason, his hand missed grabbing the rope and he fell backward twenty feet to the floor of Olympia Stadium. When he hit the ground, he landed on his heel, breaking some bones. Immediately he was put out of commission for the duration of the ice circus engagement," Delilah explains. "So I went on in his place doing the chair pyramid trick in the highwire act. After that, he would, smiling, say I stole his trick behind his back, and yet while he would say this, I could see he was very proud of me. I can still envision him the first time I did the chair trick. He sat under the wire in a wheelchair coaching me. When I finished, he handed me a dozen roses."

The next day in the newspaper, an article featured the event:

> For the first time in his 52-year career, high-wire patriarch Karl Wallenda missed a performance. . . . [He] sat by yesterday [in a wheelchair] as his teen-aged granddaughter, Delilah, took his place in the circus family's greatest and most difficult act [the chair act]. Wallenda clutched his granddaughter after she descended, amid a cheering crowd. He handed her a bouquet of long-stemmed roses. "She's got more guts than I ever had," Mrs. [Helen] Wallenda said.

To this day, Delilah keeps the newspaper clipping, which shows a picture of Vati under the wire, watching her.

The year climaxed with Karl skywalking over the Houston Astrodome. With him were Delilah, Tino, Ricky, Little Mario, Valerie, Helen, Carla, and Louie Murillo.

"He did that walk for some kind of thrill show," comments Delilah, with a shrug.

For Delilah, life on the road with Vati and Tino proved to be more and more thrilling. She feared something bad would happen and end it.

One such happening befell her that November in Sarasota. Although her Aunt Carla mourned her husband Chico's death, Carla had to move forward with her life. So she began dating and held a small family event—a cook-out. Jenny's family attended. Delilah stood around chit-chatting with relatives.

Carla asked, "Delilah, honey, how about running to the store for me and picking up some steaks?" She placed some money in her niece's hand.

Jay, Carla's friend, who'd been drinking, insisted, "I'll go, too, because I know where to get the steaks."

"I'm only going down to the corner store," countered Delilah.

"No, no, I know a another place where the steaks are better," he claimed.

Everyone looked oddly at him.

"Let him go," Carla said with a wave of her hand.

"Ja, let him go," agreed Jenny.

Jay followed Delilah to her car, carrying a bottle in one hand and a drink in another. Awkwardly he climbed in the passenger's side. Delilah put the sedan into gear, pulled out of the driveway and onto the road, keeping her eyes ahead and her mind on the steaks.

All the way, he kept making passes at her. "Come on, give me a little kiss. Go out with me. Carla won't care."

"Stop it," she said. "You're supposed to be my aunt's friend."

"Ha! She doesn't need me; she's rich now that Chico died, has all his insurance money."

"Don't talk like that," Delilah snapped. She brushed him away with her hand. "Now where is this place you claim has great steaks?"

But Jay kept up his harassment and wouldn't tell her where to go.

"Tell me where this place is," snarled Delilah, who was fed up with the drunk.

In the end Delilah went to the place she had originally intended. Jay followed her inside and picked out the most expensive meat while continuing his taunting. The more Delilah told him to stop, the worse he got. Even on the return trip, he mocked Carla while peppering his remarks with sexual innuendos.

All Delilah wanted to do was get back to her aunt's and away from him. Back in the car he began drinking again. At Tuttle Avenue, Delilah spotted some of her relatives. She tried diverting Jay's attention by calling out, "Oh look! My cousins are here!" He made a disparaging remark and she gave him a quick dirty look.

When she looked back at the road she saw a car in front of her. Instantly she slammed on the brakes.

"Jeesh!" Jay shouted as he grabbed the wheel, his cocktail glass smashing into Delilah's forehead, forcing slivers of glass into her skin and severing an artery.

Delilah groaned as blood gushed out while trying to avert

hitting the car in front of her. The collision was loud and jarring.

Afterward she moved her hand to her head to stop the still spurting blood and felt a wide gash. "I'm hurt," she mouthed, trying to remain calm.

Jay stared at her, seeing all the blood. Shaking, he spilled the bottle of liquor on her and screamed, "You're bleeding!"

"I've got to get out to see if the people in the other car are all right," Delilah whimpered.

"No," he retorted. "Look at all the blood." He restrained her.

Delilah jerked away from him and opened the door. She ran to the car in front of her. "My God," the driver said, her eyes wide. Delilah followed the woman's gaze and immediately understood her horror.

Delilah's clothing was swathed in blood.

Ambulance drivers arrived a few minutes later. Thinking that Delilah must be in shock they grabbed her and restrained her, saying, "Sit down slowly. You'll be fine."

Within seconds, they put her in the ambulance. Siren blaring, the ambulance rushed to the hospital. The paramedic stood over her, taking her blood pressure and trying to calm her. Finally they arrived and took her by stretcher to the emergency room.

To Delilah, it seemed like a long time before Jenny and Carla appeared. Doctors were stitching the artery on Delilah's forehead.

When they were finished, Delilah was left alone with Jenny. Delilah said hoarsely, "Mom, I want to tell you what happened." She quickly explained about Carla's friend.

Jenny whispered, "You should tell your aunt all this when she comes back."

Delilah sighed. "If I do, she'll be hurt because she thinks that jerk really likes her." So Delilah said nothing. The next

day word came that she'd been charged with DWI and reckless driving. "What!" she squealed. "I wasn't even drinking!" But since Carla's friend had spilled alcohol all over
her, the police thought she was driving drunk. Delilah had
to hire a lawyer.

In the past Delilah and her aunt had been close. Often
Carla had sided with Delilah when Delilah wanted to do
something and others wouldn't let her. But the accident put
a damper on their relationship. As time passed, an erosion
began. On reflection Delilah offers: "Aunt Carla was kind to
me, but I guess I always felt after that she didn't really have
it in her heart to like me."

About this time Jenny's diligent year-long investigation of
her own mother's death yielded some new information. Not
believing that her mother committed suicide, Jenny had
been conducting her own search to learn the real cause.
Everywhere Jenny had gone—from the police on down—
she'd found that no records were available that Martha had
ever died. Even a death report didn't seem to exist. Now she
heard from Joe, a family friend, that he had ridden home on
the bus with Martha right before she died. This was contra-
dictory to accounts that Martha had refused to come out of
her train car or be seen in public. Despite her mother's
sometimes strange behavior, Jenny had never believed those
accounts.

Right before her death, Jenny had received a card from
her mother saying she couldn't wait to see Jenny again.
Other stories stated that Martha had dinner with J.Y. Jenny
felt the account of her mother's unsociability were lies. How
was it that one moment Martha was supposedly too fearful
to leave her train car, and the next she was having dinner
and sitting on the bus with a friend? When the official death
report was finally discovered, it contained the most confusing elements of Martha's death. It stated that the bullet en-

tered the back of Martha's head on the left side; yet, Martha was right-handed. All who knew her felt that she couldn't have done it that way. And they wondered why J.Y. had moved her pistol to her bedside where she loaded it, when he knew she had been hospitalized not long before for a breakdown. The discrepancies were too many; Jenny continued to probe.

In 1973, Tino approached his sister and announced, "I'm getting married." Although she was happy for him, Delilah herself felt sad.

"To me, his getting married was a big thing, even though in the back of my mind, I had expected it since he and Olinka had been going together for four years," explains Delilah. "I mean, I was really losing him forever this time. All those years we had been so close, and then to think that some other woman would take priority in his life was more than I could bear. I had grown dependent on him and leaned on him for strength."

Delilah also understood that this new event might mean Tino's departure from the Wallenda troupe. He had worked for Vati so long that Vati referred to him as the "Senior Grandchild." Tino confirmed Delilah's fear.

Before Tino's wedding day, the Wallendas did a performance tour that included the Shrine Circus in Miami, a date in New Jersey, and another in Hartford in April. A month later Tino was married in Baltimore. All the Wallendas attended—even Alberto, Delilah and Tino's father, was there. A dinner party followed the exchange of vows. But while the bride and groom headed for the Poconos for their three-day honeymoon, Delilah headed in another direction to visit her mother in New York. Later she worked the Bill Kay's Shrine

Circus with Vati's performers. Here, Farrell Hetig, as well as Delilah's cousin Ricky, joined the Wallenda troupe.

When Tino returned from his honeymoon, he saw how distressed his sister was over losing him. "Look," he began. "I've been tossing around an idea. . . . I've thought up an act that could use you, so why don't you come with Olinka and me?"

Delilah shook her head. "I know you mean well, and I know Olinka wouldn't even object to my tagging along, but it's better if you start your new life without me."

Tino kissed her on the top of her head and reluctantly agreed.

About this time, Delilah began practicing a highwire motorcycle act with Louie, who had initially performed it with Tino. The first time she and Louie tried the act together, their timing was off and they got stuck upside down on the wire. It took a lot of maneuvering on Delilah's part to reseat them, and afterwards Louie told her, "Forget it, you're too light for the act." So Farrell Hetig replaced Delilah. He and Louie did the act perfectly, but it was one more reminder to Delilah that Tino was gone.

It was during this time that Karl decided to buy a brand new pickup truck. He needed one for his skywalks, and he hoped that by putting Delilah in charge of driving the equipment, she might get her mind off Tino. In addition to overseeing the equipment, Vati also put her in charge of collecting and distributing the pay. For Delilah, this gesture of Vati's faith in her at a time when she felt so badly was wonderful . . . not only did she get to perform with Vati but he also trusted her. However, Delilah's new duties didn't set well with Ricky, her cousin. A minor feud between the two teens began. It greatly saddened Delilah that Ricky—the cousin who used to sit on his Aunt Jenny's stoop early in the morning waiting to be let in, the cousin who used to stay with Delilah and Tino when his mother Carla was out performing, the cousin who Delilah felt was a second brother—now appeared competitive with her for their grandfather's affection.

Delilah felt terrible. Not only was Tino gone, but now her relationship with Ricky was going badly as well. "In 1973, Vati hired Ricky again but put me in charge of equipment and pay," Delilah says. "Ricky got mad because I was in charge. I got incensed because he got mad, attributing it to his image of the macho male who thinks since he's the man, and I am only the girl, he should be bossing me."

They butted heads en route to Wheeling from Colorado. This was Delilah's first big trip and the first major test of her new supervisory skills, so she wanted to prove to everyone that she could do it. Ricky rode ahead with a family the Wallendas knew. Everything seemed fine until Delilah heard a loud pop and the truck veered. She knew she had just blown a tire and pulled into a gas station. The tire was fixed in no time and she was back on the road, but no sooner had she caught up to Ricky and the friends than she heard a crack and THUMP-THUMP-THUMP. Wearily she pulled into a truck stop.

"Sorry," the mechanic said, shaking his head while wiping greasy hands on a white towel. "No one here can fix your tire, because we don't have one that size."

Hearing this, Ricky, who had also pulled in, walked up behind Delilah and yelled, "This wouldn't have happened if I'd been driving." They decided to go on anyway and he climbed back into the truck with her.

About a hundred miles outside of Wheeling, Delilah felt the steering wheel begin wobbling. She said to Ricky, "I don't believe it, but I think I have another flat; something's wrong."

"You can't have another flat; it's just your imagination. Keep on driving," he said forcefully.

Delilah objected, "But it feels like it. Look out the window just to make sure."

He shook his head. "Just keep driving."

When the pickup finally arrived in West Virginia, Delilah jumped out of the truck to check the tires. Her eyes widened: the rubber was gone, entirely melted; even the rim was missing. All that was left was the axle. "Look at this!" she yelled at Ricky. "If you had checked it like I wanted you to, it wouldn't have worn down to this stick!"

Another fight over an inconsequential matter escalated the bad feeling between them.

Over time, Delilah began to believe that she and Ricky were bound to remain at odds. Delilah felt that he seemed to always want the limelight, to be the important one in the family, to be the one and only one associated with Karl, nevermind that Vati had other grandchildren. Ricky remained restrained while Vati was around, but Delilah couldn't help but wonder what would happen if Vati died.

TWELVE

Love Match

Delilah could not seem to stop brooding about her brother's impending departure from both the Wallenda troupe and her life. And then, unexpectedly, something came along to fill the void. A man came into Delilah's life.

It happened in Clarksburg, West Virginia, where the troupe was appearing. Intent on getting a job done for Vati, Delilah barely noticed standing next to her a young, scruffy, unshaven crewman whom Vati had just hired on.

His name was Terry Troffer. She was introduced to him in passing. Murmured hellos were said and smiles flashed. Then Delilah walked away.

Later that day Delilah and a girlfriend hopped into the pickup truck en route to a hamburger joint. In the road, they spotted a tall, blond, well-built guy hitching a ride. "Hey, it's that new man on my grandfather's crew," said Delilah as they got closer. "I hardly recognized him cleaned up," she laughed.

"Let's give him a ride," her friend Jeanette said.

From then on, the three palled around together. Over the course of the next few months, Terry watched Delilah per-

161

form on the wire, and he was struck by how beautiful she looked, how gracefully she moved, and how courageous she was. Their palling around led to Terry asking Delilah out.

The dating lasted a year before Terry started hinting about marriage. Delilah blandly told him, "I've never seriously thought about marriage because all I've ever wanted to do and all I ever will do is work for my grandfather and do skywalks."

"Oh," Terry said, glumly accepting her rebuff at face value, at least for the moment.

In August, Vati and his people headed for New Orleans. There Terry and Delilah began seriously seeing each other. It was in New Orleans that Delilah realized how much she liked dating Terry. He didn't play silly courting games, and she always knew how he felt. It was also in New Orleans that Terry realized he was totally smitten with the petite wirewalking dynamo.

From New Orleans the troupe headed for Sarasota. With Delilah in her truck were Terry, Louie, and Cherry Fossett. What should have been a 700-mile drive—about 12 hours—turned out to take a week, because Delilah's truck kept breaking down about every 100 miles. She was very glad Terry was there, because Louie was not much comfort.

Some days later when Delilah was driving Terry home, he shyly asked her in: "Would you . . . you . . . uh, like to meet my folks?"

Delilah smiled and nodded. "Why not?" she said, climbed down from the truck, and walked into the house to meet his parents and sister Lisa. Everyone smiled at one another and said, "Hi" and "Nice meeting you." Soon Delilah returned to her truck and was on her way home to her mom's, where she had been living since Tino's marriage

Back in her old bedroom, Delilah lay down, staring at the ceiling and thinking about the tall, blond Terry. Suddenly she felt a splatter of water hit her eye. She told her mom the next morning, "The roof leaks in my bedroom, but I'll fix it."

Jenny raised an eyebrow. "You?" She decided not to object. "Well, I'm going out, so be careful."

Soon, Delilah was atop the house, amid tar, shingles, and a number of implements that she thought she needed. Her cousin Mario, who had happened by, told her not to worry. "I'll help," he called and climbed up the ladder.

After an hour or so of hard work, with their elbows in tar and their hair filled with sweat, Mario suddenly quipped, "I gotta go somewhere."

"Where?" she asked anxiously.

"Anywhere else," he laughed.

He was off, leaving her alone on the roof. Moving around to the peak of the eave, she somehow bumped the ladder, which fell flat on the ground.

"Uh-oh," she mumbled, knowing she had no way down. Sitting up there considering the situation, she suddenly felt herself sinking. Within seconds, one half of her was plunging through the roof while the other half was grasping for the sky; not only that, but tar was everywhere it shouldn't have been—on her and on the house.

Hours passed before Jenny returned and found her daughter stuck half-way in the house and half-way out, blackened and hot from the tar. "This is how you fix a roof?" her mother asked.

Delilah started crying.

The next day Terry came over and fixed the problem. His parting words to her were "Stay on the wire and not on the roof."

As the year ended, Delilah performed with the troupe on Showfolk's Circus—an annual event for the Wallendas. This was her first time performing without Tino working at her side, but Tino was there to watch her, Louie, Farrell, and

Vati perform. Seeing her brother below her, Delilah gave him a little wave, eager to show off for him and make him proud.

When the act was over and it was time for the troupe to descend the rope and take their bows, Louie was the first to go down the rope, then Farrell, and next, Delilah. Tino, forgetting that the elephants had performed right before Delilah's act, waited on the ground, ready to lift her off the rope and set her down in the ring on the ground. Delilah took a step forward, and, she says, "As Tino set me down, I slipped in their droppings right on my bottom. Tino quickly tried to catch me but mistakenly he grabbed my wig and pulled it half-way off my head. Now my head looked lopsided. And there I sat, on my rear, with my hair almost off, in front of a packed house."

In the following months, while the country's economy skidded downward, Delilah's attitude lifted as high as a helium balloon, all because she was finally performing full-time with her grandfather and engrossed in a whirlwind courtship with Terry.

The year 1975 started off with a trip to Stebbings Circus in Fort Lauderdale. Delilah noticed that Ricky seemed to have become a full-time fixture in the act. En route to Fort Lauderdale, Delilah's truck again broke down. This time it was a fan belt. Later, after ten days of selling popcorn at the fair, she had made barely enough to pay the truck's expenses. Quickly she was learning what a tough business the circus was.

On the eleventh day, she was handing a child a box of popcorn when an agonizing pain on her left side seized her. She groped her way to a chair and sat for a few minutes. Perspiring and pale, she looked up and caught sight of her new sister-in-law, Olinka, standing across from her. Delilah noticed the worry in her sister-in-law's face, but neither said anything—they were not speaking because of a family mis-understanding. Soon the pain passed, and Delilah continued manning the concession stand.

Later that afternoon, despite the soreness in her side, Deli-lah worked in Carla's unicycle act. Someone fell off the cy-cle and started a chain reaction. Like dominoes, one after another—each holding hands—the cyclists went down.

Delilah says, "I could see them going down, and when it came around for my hand to be grabbed, I quickly pulled it away, and so I ended up being the only one in the act who remained standing."

Next, the troupe headed for an appearance in Washington, D.C., with Ringling Brothers Circus, from Ashland, Ken-tucky. Delilah's truck again broke down, this time in the middle of the night. Everything was closed. Worse, it was freezing out and there was no heat in the truck. Ricky, who was riding with her, found a place to plug in the electric cord so he could try to run the heater, but this didn't work. Not wanting to freeze, they looked around and found a gas station within walking distance. Luckily it had a heated bathroom. There they spent the night, talking and keeping warm. The next day Delilah tackled fixing the truck—a chore at which she was fast becoming a pro.

With the truck working again, they got on the road and arrived in Washington, D.C., in time for their booking.

At the grounds, Delilah was surprised to see her stepfather Andy appear.

"I thought I'd stop in on my way to Flushing, where your mom is attending the funhouse."

Andy stayed with them for several days, and Delilah en-joyed his company—until one evening when, after a perfor-mance, she and Mario were walking back to their campers, talking about the act, chuckling over something funny that happened, and reviewing tomorrow's plans, each tired and hungry.

"See ya tomorrow," Mario said to his cousin as he opened the camper door. They both looked in and gasped. Inside Carla and Andy were kissing. Mario and Delilah stared at each other, shocked.

Carla mumbled over and over, "It'll never happen again."

Delilah said nothing to her mother when she first saw her, but later she decided that her mother had a right to know and told her about Andy and Carla.

When Jenny confronted Andy, he denied everything, saying, "Delilah doesn't know what she's talking about. She's crazy." Jenny kept up her accusations of her husband, and again he denied it. So Delilah asked Mario to back her up since he saw it, too.

Mario backed up Delilah's account almost word for word.

Still Andy continued to refute the accusation: "They're liars, both of them." Jenny let it blow over, but Delilah couldn't forget what she had seen.

Soon after, the troupe traveled to Syracuse, where one of the performers came down with hepatitis and everyone had to get a shot. Delilah braved it, thinking the discomfort was a lot less than the pain which still throbbed in her back and side. Not wanting to complain, she said nothing about her own discomfort; instead, she geared up for the troupe's trip to Cincinnati, where she happily admitted to herself that she was falling in love with Terry. In York, Pennsylvania, she punctuated this thought with definity: in her diary she wrote, "Yes, I'm in love."

While Delilah's relationship with Terry flourished, she also delighted in a more adult relationship with her grandfather. The more Delilah was around Vati, the more she learned about him. She found that their relationship was much different from the one she had with him when she was a little girl. Then, he used to cuddle her, hug her, balance her on his hand, bounce her on his knees. But at age twenty-one, Delilah discovered another side of her Vati. As driven and maniacal his was about his work, he was as zealous about his love for his grandchildren. Although he expressed his love for them in subtle ways, he nonetheless let them know how important they were to him and how important it was that they carry on the Wallenda name with pride.

Says Delilah, "People said he was brutal, always pushing us to perform and take unnecessary risks. Some even referred to him as the Fuehrer. But I found him to be loving."

With Delilah and the other grandchildren now in the troupe, Karl was able to take time off from practice to do some publicity. Not infrequently he flew to the next town for advance interviews while the troupe followed by truck after they'd packed up the last site. One day as he prepared to go off to do a television program, Delilah told him, "Vati, I don't feel well," and lowered her eyes to the ground, feeling guilty for not carrying her load.

Karl stared at her and then announced, "You and your mother will fly with me." He paid for their trip, put them up at a nice hotel, and said after Delilah had rested a bit, "You are well enough to do the talk shows with me, ja?"

She nodded.

"Nervous?" Vati asked.

She nodded again.

He waved his arm, "Ah, it's nothing; you'll see."

"That first show I did with him was 'The Dick Cavett Show'," says Delilah. "I remember going to New York City, and I was real nervous. And just as I was going to walk on, my mother said to me, 'Now if you say anything wrong, I'll kill you when you come back.' As I walked out to shake Dick Cavett's hand I thought about what my mother said, how she said it, and I started laughing and couldn't stop. Dick Cavett asked why I was laughing, but I thought if I told him what my mother said, she'd *really* kill me. So I didn't say anything, and I ended up feeling embarrassed. Now in looking back, I wished I had . . . at least I would have gotten a laugh out of it and not looked so dumb."

Even though she was too scared to say anything on the air that time, Karl took her to other shows because he wanted her to learn how to conduct herself as a professional showperson. After that, whenever a celebrity asked a question, Vati said, "Well, let Delilah answer that because she can do it better." Appearing in the media was just one more thing Vati taught her besides how to be an entertainer, a reliable performer, and how to take responsibility for herself. Being with him so much also showed her another side of him—a side he tried to keep hidden so as not to be taken for a softie.

Delilah explains, "He'd joke around with me all the time, and he would do special things. One time he bought me a pair of clogs, and another time he gave me a gold bracelet he bought. Other times he'd buy me charms from the places he went—to put on that gold bracelet—or he would give me a little extra money, or take me out to eat. He was just a really great grandfather. I think it's amazing he could do all those things and still run his troupe. He always seemed like a walking dynamo to me."

In 1974, the walking dynamo Karl turned seventy. Tino and Olinka were getting ready to celebrate their first anniversary. There was still a coolness between Delilah and Olinka, because it was misunderstood that Olinka's family didn't want any of Tino's relatives to visit. More tension developed, which hurt Delilah because before this dispute happened, the two young women had become close. However, because she had been told not to visit Olinka, Delilah stopped.

Meanwhile, Terry and Delilah had become more seriously involved. They spent all their spare time together. Then one night while in Baton Rouge with Karl's troupe, Terry couldn't ignore the consuming thought that he would soon lose Delilah since he was near the end of his summer tour and soon would be heading back to Sarasota while Delilah went to Cleveland. He told himself, *I'm only nineteen and she's only twenty-one, and neither of us are established financially. This relationship will never work.*

But for the love-sick Terry, logic didn't work. He worried that there were; a dozen suitors lying in waiting for the woman he loved; he decided he had to speak out. One night in Baton Rouge he said, "Since we're both getting ready to go in opposite directions, I don't want you to think I'm the kind of guy who, after spending time with a girl like you, just ups and leaves.

"No, I don't think that," she replied quietly.

"Good." He took a deep breath and blurted out, "Delilah, will you marry me?"

She answered quickly and simply, "Yes!"

"Thank God," murmured Terry, who grabbed and hugged her, dancing her around the room.

Not long after, he and Delilah shopped for an engagement ring. When they found one both liked, Terry bought it. But he prevented Delilah from putting it on, wanting to wait until he was in the car alone with her to slip it on her finger and kiss her. Delilah called her mother and said, "Terry asked me to marry him and I told him yes."

"Great, but you don't have to marry him to go to bed with him," countered Jenny.

Delilah was shocked because her mother had reared her

and Tino with strict moral values. "W-w-what do you mean?" asked Delilah.

Jenny sighed. Then there was a long pause before she asked, "Will you be content with a 'town person'?"

"What she meant by that," explains Delilah, "is a person who wasn't raised in the business, somebody from the town or private sector, especially a man who isn't likely to give up his lifestyle to join the circus. My mother knew how much I loved to perform, and she wanted me to think over what it would mean if I had to give it up to marry Terry."

"It doesn't matter," Delilah answered. "I love him so much I'll do whatever he asks of me."

"Then I'm happy for you," said Jenny, who told her husband Andy the news. However, Andy didn't like Terry and reacted unhappily. He and his wife went back and forth on it until Delilah realized her mother too had stopped caring for her fiance. Karl also didn't seem pleased about his granddaughter marrying Terry. Although Karl held his tongue, Delilah sensed that Vati would have prefered she stay with him and the highwire act.

However, with Terry at her side, the world now looked rosy to Delilah, and she waved off any discouraging comments, enjoying the heady feeling of being in love.

Not long after she got engaged, the old pain in her side worsened. The pain became so excruciating that at times she couldn't even stand up. Not wanting to complain, she tried to keep quiet about it.

However, a few weeks later, with Terry en route to his home in Sarasota and Delilah on her way to Cleveland with Ricky, things quickly grew unbearable.

In the car Delilah clutched at her side. Not noticing anything was wrong, Ricky reminded her, "Don't forget, we're supposed to do a stop in Aurora to visit my mom in Sea World."

Delilah nodded, recalling that her mother and sister Tammy are were also coming in for the visit.

Ricky drove onward while Delilah sat next to him in the passenger seat, enduring the pain. Finally, they arrived in Aurora. She was glad to see her aunt's camper. Since she felt so weak, all she could think of was lying down.

But while visiting Carla, the torment continued, searing Delilah's side like a branding iron. At last, she gave in and told her aunt, who insisted she go to a doctor.

"Just a bladder infection," the physician told Delilah, handing her some antibiotics. "It'll be better in a few days."

She nodded while her mother and aunt let out a sigh of relief. But Delilah herself was wary—because the pain was too familiar to her, she felt it couldn't be just a bladder infection. It wouldn't have lasted as long as this pain had. The ache persisted. The medication the doctor prescribed didn't help a bit.

A couple of days later, Delilah felt even worse. Jenny kept asking if she wanted to go to the hospital, but Delilah insistently shook her head, gritting her teeth with the pain.

Then, at 5:00 A.M., Delilah awakened with such fierce, sharp pain that she wanted to vomit. Delilah called to her mother for help. Looking at Delilah's face and writhing body, Jenny immediately took her to Brentwood Hospital's emergency room.

There Delilah saw new doctors who repeatedly questioned her. "You've never had this pain before?" they kept asking.

She muttered, "Nothing as bad as this."

The doctors admitted her to the hospital and ran a slew of tests. The pain continued, so harrowing now that she passed out while being X-rayed, hitting her head and skinning her knee.

Still trying to ascertain what was wrong, the doctors continued their questioning: "Have you ever fallen off the wire and hit your side?"

Just as insistently, she countered, "No, never."

"Could you have hit something?" a doctor asked. "Maybe rammed your side into something?"

Delilah shook her head. "The only thing I've ever done is fall off a curb once when I was a kid."

The doctor shrugged. "We'll need to run more tests."

They came up with every feasible cause for her pain but the right one. A young internist thought it might be a birth defect; another resident said she had probably fallen and didn't know it. To Delilah, who was suffering, they seemed to be taking forever to discover what was wrong with her.

Finally, one morning several days later, a distinguished-looking, gray-haired physician named John Frohme walked over to her hospital bed and said, "Well, at last we can make a diagnosis; you have a serious kidney infection. It looks like you've had it since childhood."

"And that's why I keep getting this pain in my side?" Delilah asked amazed.

Dr. Frohme nodded. "But because it never got taken care of, the infection also went into your other kidney, and that's why the pain's been so severe."

With medication, the doctors began to get the infection in one kidney under control.

Meanwhile Mario learned from his mother Carla about Delilah's illness; so he called Terry, who immediately hitched a ride to Cleveland to see his sick fiancee.

"I was never so happy to see someone as I was him," she says. "It meant a lot to me that he came right away."

"Are you really going to be okay?" he asked.

Seeing the worry on his face, the fear in his eyes, and knowing that after traveling all the way home to Sarasota, he turned around and went right to Cleveland because his wife-to-be was in the hospital, lifted Delilah's spirits.

Still the hospital tests went on and on. Finally a doctor told her, "We'd like to try and save the bad kidney. But it may take a while, so you would be better off going back home to Sarasota and seeing a doctor there."

Tired of endless tests and hospitalization, Delilah decided to follow his instructions. Terry and Delilah flew home, and Terry's parents picked them up at the airport. It was only the second time Delilah had met his family. Worried about Delilah, and not really knowing her, the Troffers said little, and Delilah was afraid they didn't like her. They took her to Karl and Helen's house to stay, because Jenny was away.

After getting settled at Mutti Helen's, Delilah realized she still did not feel at all that well and, following the Cleveland doctor's suggestions, she made an appointment with a urologist. At his office, he did still another internal exam and studied the X-rays from Brentwood Hospital. He decided to run only one test. Based on this single test, he turned to Delilah and said, "Your kidney needs to be removed. When would you like it done? Tomorrow? Next week? Next month? No big deal . . . have the surgery whenever it suits you."

She left his office in tears. She says, "I was stunned—so stunned that I said nothing. Worse, I believed in him, thought he knew what he was doing, that he had done everything he humanly should have before wanting to cut me open and remove this vital organ, and he acted as if the procedure was no more important than having a mole removed."

Since Terry couldn't see the doctor with her, and Jenny was on her way to Flushing, Delilah was left alone to make a decision that would affect her the rest of her life. She told him she needed time. Frightened and crying, she rushed to

Helen's house and told her. Helen didn't know what to do to help.

Then the phone rang. On the other end was Jenny eager to find out what the doctor had to say. Delilah was crying so hard she could hardly tell her. "What?" Jenny said into the phone. "Delilah, I can't understand anything you're saying because you're hysterical." After finally ferreting out the story, Jenny became frantic. She hung up and called her stepfather J.Y. to see if he could get Delilah into the Mayo Clinic, since he was friends with the Mayo family.

Soon Jenny called Delilah back. "You're going to be examined at the Mayo Clinic, where some of the world's best doctors are. If anyone can help you, they can."

"But what about my wedding plans?" Delilah began sobbing.

"Your kidney is more important. It might mean your life."

Delilah murmured, "I know," and prepared herself for more tests and probing.

At the clinic, with her family standing by, Delilah underwent more tests. Days later, a team of doctors circled her bed and informed her, "We have to operate, but we think we can save the kidney."

They scheduled her for surgery, and on that day a sedated but frightened Delilah was wheeled into the operating room. Hours later, the complicated procedure was completed. The surgeons threw off their surgical masks and gloves and walked out of the operating room. The gray-haired doctor looked for the mother of his patient. As he approached, Jenny and Andy, who were also there, rose, their faces carry expressions of fear and distress.

"Well," he began. "She's made it through the surgery very well."

They sighed.

"But," he added, "when we got in there we saw that the

bad kidney was four times its normal size with a hole as large as a half-dollar, leaving little good tissue. There was nothing we could do to save it. We had to remove it."

Jenny said fearfully, "But she's all right?"

He smiled. "She's fine. Being young, she'll be able to handle this."

By the evening of her operation, Delilah was up walking around. Three days later, she was discharged from the hospital. In five days, she was flying home to Sarasota.

But within a few days of being back home with her mother, she began feeling ill again. That night she tossed restlessly, feeling hot and sweaty. By dawn she was wide awake and looked down to see her nightgown was soaked with pus. Moaning, she managed to sit up.

She called the doctor who had first seen her when she returned from Mayo but he couldn't see her. "It's urgent. My incision's infected," she implored him.

He told her to get an appointment with his partner, who saw her and tended to the infection, which finally cleared up.

Though she was slowly getting better, Delilah felt weighted down by illness and depression. Adding to her woes, she found out she'd already been replaced in the troupe by Carla's daughter Rietta. Delilah explains, "It wasn't as though we all knew I would be out of work for a while. The second I'm absent, Aunt Carla replaces me with her daughter. She could have at least waited to see how sick I was, if I'd be out of work for a long time, or when I could return to my job. It was like the minute I turn my back, my place gets stolen from me."

Delilah felt that her life was filled with trial and trouble. To ease that burden, she continued her search for some higher meaning to its struggles. She went to prayer meetings, reading the Bible, trying to learn in what direction the Lord wanted her to go.

In June, the birth of Tino and Olinka's first child—whom they named Alida—was perhaps the best news of the difficult year. On hearing about it, Delilah broke into smiles. "I'm an aunt," she said proudly.

T HIRTEEN

New Beginnings

As 1974, a year filled with illness and pain, passed and a new one was poised on the horizon, Delilah finally had reason to rejoice. Her and Terry's wedding date was drawing near. They were both ready for the happy event. However, like all weddings, their's had the usual tension . . . and then some. The first problem was Andy, who was supposed to give Delilah away at Concordia Lutheran Church.

He and Terry had a disagreement right after Christmas. Andy threw Terry out of the house, yelling, "I'm not going to any wedding—let alone give Delilah away!" And he shattered into hundreds of pieces the Christmas gift given to him by the betrothed couple. "Never again is he allowed in my house," Andy added, pointing to Terry.

Delilah tried not to be too upset—she had wanted Tino to give her away anyway.

When Andy didn't attend the wedding rehearsal Delilah was sure he wouldn't be at the wedding the next day either. Her bridesmaids included Jeannette Rix, Klara Valla, Tosca Kora, Catherine Mulizza, and M.J. Troffer. Flower girls were Delilah's half-sisters. Farrell Hettig was Terry's best man, while ushers included J.P. Arnosie, Tom Troffer, Mario, and Camp Douglas. Giovanni Zoppe—Delilah's half-brother—was to be the ring bearer. Tino walked her down the aisle, and the rehearsal went off without a problem.

The next morning, Delilah awoke to her wedding day. January 6th hadn't rolled around fast enough for her. At last her existence was complete and she was embarking on a new life with the man she was devoted to. Four hundred people jammed the church.

"Ready?" Tino asked his sister, the organ music cuing him. He extended his arm to Delilah to usher her down the aisle.

She smiled at him, and then turned toward the church passageway.

Suddenly, up popped Andy, dressed in a tuxedo. "I'm doing this," he said definitively, holding his elbow out for Delilah. "After all, I'm your stepfather, and I am the one paying for the wedding."

For a moment, Delilah considered chucking everything and taking off with Terry to elope, but then she focused on her main concern, Terry, with whom she was getting ready to exchange vows. Her husband-to-be was everything she'd ever wanted in a man and looked so princely as he nervously waited for his bride to join him. She obediently took Andy's arm.

The wedding service went off without any further calamity, but the reception did not. The four hundred people, who had fit comfortably in the large church, packed every inch of space at the Showfolks Club in Sarasota. They mingled, ate finger foods, talked to one another, laughed, danced, and drank more and more champagne.

"When are all these people going to leave?" a jittery Terry finally whispered to his new wife. "I don't know anyone here."

"The reception just started," Delilah answered, a grin on her face. "But we'll go early. It won't be long."

Jenny floated by the newlyweds, saying, "Open your presents."

Terry shook his head. "That's not proper. I wasn't taught that way. We'll do that in the privacy of our home."

"No, open them now," insisted Jenny. "That's what you're supposed to do.

They argued loudly.

"Stop it, both of you!" Delilah cried, trying to keep her voice low. But then everyone stopped what they were doing to listen. Nervously, Delilah ripped open a present just to quiet her mother, splitting a nail in the process and getting blood on her wedding gown.

"How could you do that to her!" Terry yelled at his mother-in-law.

Abashed and angry, Jenny hollered back, "That's it! I wash my hands of you!" and she walked out of the hall and went home. For months, she and her daughter didn't talk, and when they finally did, it was only because Delilah initiated it. Since then, neither Terry nor Delilah like to discuss their wedding.

But their marriage was a good one, and their love strengthened with each passing day. Delilah reflects, "After I got married, I had a certain strength that I think came to me through Terry, who had a very solid belief in God." Delilah began to read the Bible daily.

In May, she and Terry visited a Christian coffee house in St. Petersburg, Florida, where alcohol and drugs were taboo. Soda and food were offered along with ministrations to the Lord. Delilah and Terry sat at a table, quietly talking. Suddenly Delilah saw a young man from the band rising.

"Ladies and gentlemen," he began.

Inclining her head, Delilah listened to him.

179

"I know there's someone in the audience who has accepted Christ into her heart as her Savior, but Satan keeps telling her that she isn't good enough to live Christ's life. Whoever this person is, I want you to imagine yourself driving an iron stake right now into the ground to mark it as the day Christ has accepted you for who you are, and that your sins are forgiven and you're entitled to go to Heaven." With his voice intensifying, he went on: "I want you always to remember this moment as the day you were really saved."

"He's talking about me!" Delilah murmured to Terry.

Delilah offers, "I broke into sobs, elated that someone understood how I felt and then went further by telling me how to fix my problem. Terry, who was by my side, clasped my hand. Terry's strength came through, and with his love and God's love, I knew everything would be all right—both on the highwire and in my life."

From then on, Delilah felt that her existence was finally complete.

Later an article about Delilah came out in the *Lewiston Morning Tribune*. She was asked if she feared the wind the most. She answered, "Performers always worry about high winds when having to walk a skinny wire, but we don't let the wind rule our lives. We have to go up and perform no matter how drafty it is—it's our job. The verbal rule is that the show must go on, but we have to use common sense, too. No one wants to see us kill ourselves up there. But yet, one can't perform if he or she has fear. Respect for the wire is one thing; fear is another." She added, "Yes, I could be killed, [but] I could be killed crossing the street [too]. I trust in the Lord. I'm a born-again Christian. We live our lives for Jesus."

* * *

Despite Delilah's new-found spirituality and serenity, however, one serious problem still did exist. It was a financial one: Although Jenny had paid off the Mayo account, Terry and Delilah still had to pay the Cleveland hospital bill and other expenses of Delilah's illness. So the Troffers started their marriage seriously in debt. To help offset this, Terry officially began his wirewalking career in New Orleans.

Having practiced on the lowwire before, he was no stranger to the cable. So when he was needed, Terry was right up there with his wife, balancing the act. When there wasn't work for him or Delilah, they returned to Sarasota, where they worked in Terry's dad's waterproofing business or Delilah waitressed at the Shrine Club or cleaned house for Mutti Helen. They made some progress but remained in debt. To help ameliorate this Delilah signed up as a cook's helper at a local restaurant. In the meantime, when they could find time, she and Terry practiced a hanging perch act; later, they bought some rigging from Carla.

"Around this time," begins Delilah, "my grandfather approached Terry and me and asked if we would like to work for him. But it would mean, added Vati, that Terry would have to go one place for awhile to set up Grandfather's skywalks while Vati and I would end up working the highwire with the troupe at other sites."

Terry and Delilah discussed the proposition at length, and because they needed the money and wirewalking was their career, they took Vati up on his offer. Over the next few months Terry found himself flying or driving back and forth from one state to another, setting up or dissembling the rigging for Karl's skywalks, while Delilah worked elsewhere on the wire with Louie, Farrell, Rietta, and others. Sometimes she stayed in hotels; other times she lived in Karl's camper.

Because Delilah and Terry lived in a mobile home in Sarasota, they didn't have a trailer to travel from job to job, so Vati gave them his while he went out and bought a new one. And although they were tight-lipped about their financial status, wise old Karl and his wife Helen knew differently. Over the years, and especially since Mutti Martha's death, Helen had tried to substitute as a grandmother for Delilah and Tino. Periodically she'd do special things that made Delilah respect her all the more, such as the time when everyone but the Troffers were going on R&R.

"Isn't it great!" said one of the troupe members. "Karl's giving us three days off, and we're all going to a campground for fun and relaxation."

"Yeah, I wish we could," Delilah sighed heavily, knowing she and Terry wouldn't be joining them because they didn't have money.

Somehow knowing this, Helen quietly went over to Delilah and handed her some money saying, "Here, take this, and join everyone at the campground." After she crumpled the bills into her step-grandchild's hand, she whispered, "But don't tell your grandfather."

Delilah grinned and kissed Helen, loving her at that moment every bit as much as she had loved her natural grandmother.

An hour later, Vati crept over and shoved something into Delilah's hand. "Don't tell your grandmother," he said and walked away. Delilah stared at another handful of money. Now, instead of not going at all, she and Terry were able to spend two nights at the campground.

A short while after the mini-vacation, Vati offered her a job at Six Flags Over Texas in Arlington. The Troffers stayed there the entire summer, performing for Karl, who had two highwire acts going. In one act the Troffers worked with Ferrell Hettig. The other consisted of Ricky, his sister Rietta, another man, and Karl himself, who traveled to various engagements. The summer proved to be trying for the soon-to-be 24-year-old Delilah, who began feeling ill and exhausted much of the time. Not knowing why, she was glad their engagement at Six Flags was coming to an end.

But when she and Terry returned to home base in Sarasota, Vati approached them, saying, "I need you to replace Rietta, who has to return to school." This, of course, meant traveling again.

They agreed, although Delilah, feeling constantly tired, spent most of her free time napping. By September, right around Labor Day, she learned her symptoms weren't a recurrence of her kidney problem but rather a manifestation of pregnancy. Ecstatic, the Troffers spent their nights thinking of boys' and girls' names. Terry, typical of most fathers-to-be, fretted around his wife, worrying about her climbing and walking the wire. But Delilah insisted on carrying on.

Reflects Delilah, "I ended up performing until I was six months pregnant. Everybody told me not to stop practicing. Now I know why. I had that week off and didn't practice, and by the time I got to Cleveland, I started to look pregnant. Before that, I had been wearing my usual clothes, even though they were a little tight around the waist. But after I quit practicing I had to buy a whole new wardrobe. I remember going up in the elevator one day when someone said to me, 'My goodness! I just see how you've grown overnight!' The only trick I ended up doing on the wire was putting my knee down on the shoulder bar."

During the rest of her pregnancy she and Terry attended birthing classes. By her seventh month, Delilah was beginning to bewail her ungainly shape, grumbling to Terry, "I'm getting to be as big as a house!"

"At least it's temporary," he said, thinking his words would console her.

Delilah repeated her concerns to her gynecologist, adding, "I think you've miscalculated, and the baby's due sooner."

The doctor raised his eyebrows. "Miscalculate? I've been a doctor longer than you've been alive, and I'm telling you this baby's not going to be born before March."

Delilah, used to obeying, nodded.

On February 9th, she was on her knees washing Helen's kitchen floor as part of her cleaning job and felt her stomach protruding. *I'm huge,* she thought, pondering her doctor's words—another month to go. She was sure she'd explode by then. She finished her work and went home. That night, she and Terry attended another birthing class. The next morning she awoke and made lunch for Terry to take to work. Standing at the kitchen counter, she felt a strange sensation and looked down.

"Oh Terry!" she cried out as her water broke.

Terry took her in his arms and then they headed for the hospital, where the doctor examined her and informed her, "You're not ready for the baby to be born; if it is, you'll be lucky it weighs five pounds."

"But I still think you're a month off with your calculations," Delilah objected.

"I think not," the doctor tossed her comment off. Eventually, however, because her membranes had broken, he decided to induce labor.

Four hours later, Delilah gave birth to a 7-pound, 15-ounce baby girl. The doctor looked at the normal sized baby and said, "Well, she's certainly not a preemie; we'll just say she's full-term."

Delilah shook her head, knowing all along she had been correct.

A few days later the Troffers brought the baby home, and

soon nearly all the Wallendas were arriving at their door, eager to see this new addition to the family. Vati and Mutti Helen bought her a crib, while Martha's widowed husband, J.Y., made a request: "Would you name the baby after your Mutti Martha?" Terry and Delilah agreed, calling her Lijana Adina Martha Troffer. Holding her, Delilah thought how beautiful her baby was, although she was the first to admit, "She does look like all babies when they're first born—you know, kind of from outer space. And she's totally bald."

With three in the family now, the Troffers soon found they didn't have enough room in Vati's tiny old trailer. They were worried. They'd have to buy a new one, which would put them deeper in debt. Noticing their distress, Karl offered to buy one for them and let them pay him instead of having to take out a bank loan. They breathed easier.

Just as they saw themselves escaping from this financial pressure another one surfaced. Delilah and Terry discovered that there was something wrong with Lijana's legs; they took her to a specialist, who put the three-month-old in a cast. Hearing this, Tino sent his sister some money to help pay the doctor, but in spite of his help, their medical bills kept mounting. With all these financial worries, Delilah knew she couldn't stay home. She says, "The world doesn't come to a standstill because a woman has a baby. In order to eat and pay bills, I had to go back to work."

Soon after, she and Terry were scheduled to perform out west, but the doctor told them that Lijana's cast had to come off in six weeks and that after that she'd need special shoes for another six weeks. Delilah felt overwhelmed and told the doctor. Understanding their situation, the doctor gave them the shoes.

In the next months, Delilah and Terry performed for Vati and did their act for other circuses in such places as Idaho, Colorado, West Virginia, and Ohio. Lijana, whose bones were strengthening, stood in Terry's and Vati's hands, never-mind that she could not yet sit, crawl, or walk. She was a Wallenda and thus could naturally balance herself.

Although Delilah felt increasingly tired trying to fulfill all her different responsibilities, she was satisfied. She loved her family, and all the Wallendas were getting along. Still, Delilah looked forward to a respite. However, just when it appeared they would finally get one, Vati announced that a major movie special was in the works. It was to be called "The Great Wallendas." The clincher was that the clan had to re-create the seven-man pyramid.

Delilah says, "We got home and started practicing the seven-man pyramid for the movie. It was a lot of fun work-ing with that many people on the highwire at the same time. I tried out for Jana's part, but the casting director said I was too shy, so I didn't get it, but Terry did get a part, which meant more income for us." Britt Ekland played Jenny, but when the character Jenny was supposed to be on the highwire, Delilah did the stunts for Britt. Lloyd Bridges was cast as Karl. The film promised to be a spellbinding account of the seven-man tragedy. However, production on the movie was held up because of negotiations with Ron Morris, who wrote *Karl Wallenda*. The producer had read Morris's book and wanted to use it as the backup source for the movie. The two went back and forth on the deal. Morris explains, "All of the information in the movie came out of my book. It took me almost a year to figure out the Wallenda lineage and do all the research, and then another two years to write the book, as well as put up with all the jealousy in the family." Morris adds, "Some of the other Wallendas stopped talking to me after the book came out. My biggest problem was Karl; I could never get him to sit down and talk to me."

Finally, Morris and the producer struck a deal. The first

two weeks of filming were done in Vati's backyard in Sarasota, more footage was shot on the beach, other shootings took place in Manasota Memorial Garden, where Dick and Dieter were buried, and still more footage was done in Sarasota Memorial Hospital.

Besides doing the movie, Terry, Delilah, and Tino also worked on the "PTL Club" show. For Delilah, life was thrilling! She noticed Vati also seemed to be having a good time. However, Delilah felt he was becoming unstoppable in his compulsion to top even himself. "There's not a height that could push me back," he said boasting in the *News Register*. Then in the *Lewiston Morning Tribune* he remarked, "After 50 feet, it doesn't matter how high you are. . . . I'd walk a cable 10,000 feet high, if they could put it up. I fall 50 feet, I'm dead anyway."

Finally, filming for "The Great Wallendas" ended, and everyone relaxed. Some of the troupe pursued other interests: Dave Klukow, a friend of Terry and Delilah's who had been performing in the group, left the Wallendas and went to Bible school; Ricky headed for Germany to work with Youth With a Mission; others just took time off for rest and relaxation from the wire.

That the furor of filming was at last done was especially good news for Delilah, who by then badly needed to get some rest. The movie plus outside commitments and her duties as a wife and mother had taken a lot out of her. Finally she was able to take some time off, but as the weeks passed and no amount of sleep seemed to help her recover, she decided to see a doctor. He told her that she was again pregnant.

Once again, Terry and Delilah went through lists of

names, trying to find the right one for their new baby, and they reviewed their plans for the future in an attempt to decide whether they should go back on the road or stay at home for a while. They prayed hard, asking the Lord for guidance and direction. His answer, they thought, was for them to start their own two-person act; so they told Vati they were leaving the troupe to do their own act. He was excited for them and urged that they use the Wallenda name, as it was good promotion for him, too. So the Troffers began practicing their own act, the two-high.

Feeling confident in their decision, Delilah went through her days like a trooper. Nothing seemed to bother her, certainly not pregnancy. Besides, she worked while pregnant with the last baby and everything had turned out all right, and this time she was healthier and more careful.

Yet a few weeks later, she was having heavy cramps and suspected something was wrong. She grew more and more disturbed about it, because she had prepared for this baby, her kidney problem was behind her, and she had been resting. Yet she put her concerns aside when Vati visited one night to ask a favor.

"I have work for you to do," he told her and Terry. "Since Ricky has gone to Germany, I can't call on him to do it, and I can't do it because I'm doing a highwire act in Puerto Rico."

"By yourself, Vati?" Delilah asked. For some reason she was momentarily worried.

Vati waved her concerns away. "Rietta and a couple of men on the crew will go with me. But I need another act to perform in the States, in Omaha. What I need for you to do is to serve as my second act in Omaha."

Terry and Delilah felt that after all Vati had done for them, they owed it to him to help him out. Despite Delilah's worries over her pregnancy, they agreed.

Afterward, they had mixed emotions, but because they'd committed themselves to Karl, they began practicing for the Omaha date.

On their third day of practice, Delilah started bleeding. She telephoned a doctor and got an appointment. She explains, "I went to a doctor who was cheaper than the gynecologist I usually see because in addition to paying on the Cleveland hospital bill and others, we were then paying for Lijana's bill—a never-ending cycle."

"I think I'm miscarrying," she told the doctor.

"Get an appointment with me in two weeks and stay in bed until then," he advised. "And send me my money in advance."

Delilah didn't like the mercenary tone of the physician, but she followed his advice.

The hardest part was having to tell Vati she couldn't do his dates. Delilah told Karl, "Vati, I have to stay in bed for at least two weeks so that I won't miscarry; I can't do the Omaha engagement for you."

She says, "I remember seeing the hurt in his eyes, but he didn't say anything to me, just nodded as though he understood. But later I heard that he didn't really believe that I had started to miscarry. He figured that I didn't want to work for him any longer and that I was giving him the shaft, that Terry and I were just trying to get out of our agreement."

Trying to recover her strength, Delilah spent the next week at her mother-in-law's house, but Jenny got upset because she wanted to take care of her daughter. Knowing how strained Terry and her mother's relationship was, Delilah realized going to Jenny's house wouldn't work either. So the second week Delilah returned to her own home, where the ladies from her church helped out by cleaning the house, taking care of Lijana, and bringing meals in.

Finally, on a cold January morning, it was time to see the physician. Terry's mother drove Delilah to the doctor's office for her appointment. The doctor curtly ushered Delilah into the examining room and did an internal on her and just as quickly dismissed her with a wave of his hand and a final word: "Continue to stay in bed, and I want the remainder of the money before the baby's born."

Delilah gave him all the money she had and left his office in tears.

"What's wrong?" Terry's mom asked, following her daughter-in-law to the car.

Delilah told her. Mrs. Troffer stomped back into the doctor's office, demanded that the doctor return the money, and told him he'd get paid for delivery of the baby when it was born and not a minute sooner.

The next day, Delilah miscarried.

At her regular gynecologist's office, Delilah confessed, crying, "I didn't go to you because of our money problems."

"Next time, you come *here*, and don't worry about the bill," he told her. Then, softening his tone, he added, "The internal exam that other doctor gave you is something that shouldn't be done when there's possibility of a miscarriage. I have to admit you to the hospital for a D&C to make sure nothing's left inside you."

Distraught over losing her baby, Delilah kept to herself for days. When word got out that Delilah had lost her baby, everyone felt badly, but no one felt worse than Vati. He blamed himself for not believing his granddaughter. In the end, Tino and little Mario, Ricky's younger brother, had to replace Terry and Delilah in the Omaha engagement, while Vati went off to Puerto Rico to perform on the highwire.

___FOURTEEN

A Time of Endings

Yes, sometimes [I get afraid], on the night before. Once I have taken the first step onto the wire, I am thinking of only getting to the other side . . . then when I have walked the wire, I have two strong martinis and I forget it. . . .

What matters is whether you *need* to walk the wire. You must be a little afraid, and you must want to prove that you are not afraid. . . .

I want to have control over a situation. If I die, I want it to be my fault.

—Karl Wallenda[27]

While Delilah rested at home, she heard that Vati was going to do an unplanned skywalk in Puerto Rico. She felt oddly about this stroll across a 300-foot-long, silvery wire strung between the roofs of two beach-front hotels—a wire no thicker than the width of a man's finger. What bothered her was that the skywalk had come about so quickly that

Vati had to borrow equipment to do it since he had originally gone to San Juan to do a regular highwire booking. Why this skywalk should bother her, she didn't understand. She knew her grandfather had done many with no problems. Vati had walked a wire strung 750 feet across the canyon at Tallulah Gorge, as well as one strung 640 feet over Veterans Stadium in Philadelphia, so this one in San Juan should have been a cakewalk to him in comparison, even if he was 73. Though he had had heart surgery, he was now recovered and his body was strong and firm as a man of twenty-five. He had also been walking the wire for over fifty-seven years, performing worldwide in the best and the ugliest of situations.

Delilah knew he was *the* expert, being able to tell if the weather was right, what size wire he needed, how much his pole should weigh and how long it had to be. But she felt a twinge of fear nevertheless. She was still wondering what had happened in the seven-man tragedy. As the time for the skywalk drew near, Delilah could not stop thinking about Vati. She remembered what her Uncle Mario had said: "My father knows what can happen up there on the wire, but he doesn't let it bother him because it is the only thing in life for him. What else could he do for a living? The wire is his living and his life," yet for some reason, despite Mario's words and all she knows about Vati's skill, Delilah could not stop worrying. After all, Vati was only human and he too could make mistakes.

Southeast of Sarasota, sandwiched between the Atlantic Ocean and the Carribean Sea in San Juan, another person brooded about Vati's skywalk. A number of times Helen had pleaded with her husband to put it off, as had other relatives and friends and even Karl's press agent, Stephanie Shaw, who contended, "There's no way to measure the updraft or the gusts of wind from the sea. Do it some other time."

But he simply responded, "I gave my word to a man I've known a long time." Helen kept trying to make Karl give up on the walk.

He reassured her: "It's just a breeze. I've made longer walks in worse winds."

And those longer walks, just as the one he was going to do for San Juan, were without a net. Karl believed nets gave wirewalkers false confidence and often resulted in more severe injuries because highwire aerialists bounced out as soon as they hit. Some claimed, though, that Karl did these things so that his acts would be even more exciting.

With Karl and Helen in San Juan were three of his students—Rietta Wallenda, his granddaughter by Carla, and two understudies: Farrell Hetig and Philip Gikas. The three went sightseeing in San Juan the night before the performance, while Karl and Helen strolled around hand-in-hand like school children, chatting and carrying on.

That night Helen tried to get him to change his mind, but he grew all the more adamant and committed to the walk. "Everything will be fine; you'll see. Don't worry," he reassured her. Since the seven-man pyramid had fallen in Detroit, Helen had chosen not to watch Karl's death-defying walks. She went to bed that evening feeling troubled.

The next morning, Karl rose, beaming and eager to begin his day. He checked outside, noting that it was a windy day for a walk suspended 120 feet above the ground where gusts averaged 30 M.P.H. "The wind is my worst enemy," he once said at an outdoor performance, and yet he walked the wire in severe tempests.

According to a *Sarasota Herald Tribune* article the circus was sold out that morning.[28] Two hours before the show was about to start, Helen took Karl to their hotel window and pointed to the crowds below; they were lined up for blocks. "Why, Karl?" she asked. "You don't need to do this."

However, Karl didn't listen. He was thinking only of doing the skywalk.

Next, Helen went to the promoter of the circus and asked him to stop the skywalk, but he refused. She tried the hotel owner, but he didn't want to get involved either. No one seemed to want to help her save her husband. She knew Karl prided himself on giving an audience its money's worth. She didn't believe he had a death wish, yet he was fatalistic. He had once told her that he would perform as long as the good Lord let him. When she had asked how he would know that, he replied, "When he leaves me, I'll know."

At ground level, the breeze was blowing at 12 M.P.H. Someone mentioned to Karl, "Maybe it's too windy for your suspension walk."

But he only smiled.

Helen accompanied her husband to the hotel room where he was to begin his walk, then left and sat in her room away from the window, dark thoughts passing through her mind. Rietta and Philip remained at ground level, amidst a crowd of spectators. Farrell went to the inn room across from them where the walk would then end.

Karl continued with his preparations, seeming to consider this walk to be nothing more than routine.

Sometime after eleven that breezy morning, Karl stepped out on the wire over Ashford Avenue carrying a 35-pound, 25-foot pole. Immediately the crowd went silent. He took a few steps forward. The wind rushed through the wind tunnel made by the two hotels and slammed into him.

Another gust of wind whipped through him. He took one step, and then paused. The crowd was so quiet that the wind's menacing hiss could be heard battering Karl about. Determined, he moved forward again. All along the line he did this—a step forward, then a pause—until he got just about midway. Then he stopped.

The wind unrelentingly taunted him, ballooning his shirt, blowing his pants, ripping into his face, cutting off his breath. He kept at it, took another ten or fifteen steps, and then he bent his knees as if to curl up from the wind, yet lean into it. The wire vibrated under his feet like a strummed guitar string.

Someone heard Rietta yell from the ground, "Sit down, Grandfather, sit!"

Karl crouched, yelling at the nine-man crew, "Tighten it! Tighten it!"

A sudden burst of wind jarred him, his foot slipped out, his expression changed into surprise, and he desperately grabbed for the wire.

He clung to it for a split-second with his right hand, his left still holding the pole—"Never, ever drop the pole"—and then, unable to hold the wire any longer, he let go of the wire and grabbed the pole, falling with it while holding it in the professional wire-walking position. The wind buffeted him even as he tumbled. Straight down he went, he and his pole slicing through the air. He slammed into the roof of a taxi, bounced off and hit the sidewalk hard. He died of massive internal injuries.

Upstairs in the hotel room, his wife heard the shrieks outside. Then she heard the pounding on the door, sounding much like the pounding in her heart. When she finally forced herself to get up and open the door, she saw Rietta standing before her.

"He fell," Helen said flatly.

Rietta said yes.

"He's dead?"

Again Rietta said yes and clutched Helen in her arms.

In her grandfather's honor, Rietta, Farrell, and Philip did a matinee that very afternoon as a way of saying how much they loved and respected Karl.

That night, Carla, Rietta's mother, flew to Puerto Rico with Jenny and a family friend.

Back in Sarasota, Delilah's phone rang. Delilah says softly: "I remember how I got the news of Grandfather's death. When my mother called me, I could tell by her voice that something bad had happened. There are no words for my shock, my pain; no one thought he'd ever fall, that he too was vulnerable. He was my teacher. I loved him so much."

The iron-tough patriarch was loved by more than just the Wallendas—the world loved him, too, for his courage, his perseverance, his physical and emotional strength.

The casket was flown from San Juan free of charge, courtesy of the airline. Wanting to say goodbye to their hero, Americans packed Robarts Arena where Karl's body lay in state.

Three different ministers attended: a rabbi, a priest, and a Protestant minister.

Helen offers, "After Karl fell, we got flowers from all over the world. They were so many flowers coming in that we had them sent to Robarts, where they were arranged on the stage. There were two big arrangements right in the middle, the biggest ones of all. They had been sent by the promoter and the hotel owner. I found an attendant and told him I wanted those flowers removed from the building. I wanted them out of my sight. He asked where he should put them. I said, 'You have a big dumpster out back, don't you? That's where I want them.' "[29]

Limosines shunted the family to and from the crowded arena; Karl's children were in one limosine, the grandchildren in another. Mobs of people who had seen Karl wanted to say goodbye. It seemed everyone wanted to claim a part of Karl. There was much confusion on everyone's part, including the owner of the funeral home, who drove the limousines: She locked the family in the limo and couldn't figure out how to get them out. Finally the problem was resolved when someone found another key.

Gunther and Andy stood guard at the coffin. Suspended over the casket was Karl's balancing pole. A constant flow of people streamed through Robart's. Mario offers, "Even my father's funeral was like a circus." He believes his dad died happily, saying, "My father's friend Jack had a stroke, and I remember my father telling me that he wouldn't want to be like that because if he had to, he'd rather be dead. My father wanted to go out in a blaze of glory; he didn't want to die in bed. He went fast. Anybody who falls ten stories goes fast."

Helen agrees with this. "I remember walking through a park with him and seeing an old man sitting on a bench. Karl told me he never wanted to be like that, feeble and worn out. He used to say, 'Whoever said growing old is a privilege should have had his head examined.' "[30]

Amid all this, the grandchildren met to talk about the future.

Offers Delilah, "I remember we had all gotten together to discuss who should fulfill the rest of Vati's contracts, with the money going to Mutti, but I don't know why we had this discussion since Helen had already asked Tino, my brother. But my cousins Rietta and little Mario ran back to Helen saying Tino and I were cutting them off; so Helen canceled everything. In the end, it didn't matter, since word got out that she had told Ricky he was going to be the one to do them anyway."

Not only who would succeed Karl, but learning the cause of death was important to the Wallenda family. Offers Delilah, "None of us believed he could have fallen. . . . I mean, this man was *the* expert highwire walker. In fact, we all insisted on reviewing the videotape of his fall just to be sure it was really him, just to see what could have possibly gone wrong. Plain and simple it was human error: someone didn't attach the guywires properly."

Accounts vary, but Delilah believes her grandfather never checked the guy wires. "After all, he had a crew of men running the cables. Although this was the first time one of them ever worked for Vati, the other had been with our company for a long time, and he should have known exactly what to do."

She, along with a few other relatives, couldn't help but feel that one of the men erred in rigging the wires between the buildings.

"When it happened," adds Delilah, "everyone said, 'Don't say anything,' but I thought the guy who made the mistake needed to know. I needed to know if it was human error or something even less correctable and therefore more frightening."

Mario agrees with his niece. "The guy wires were all wrong; someone didn't properly tie the guy line to the cable. My father had other people setting up that day. There was none of the family there to do it properly. His riggers were ultimately responsible for checking all the guy wires."

But his wife Linda attributes the tragedy to more than a mistake in setting up. "Karl was too good of a walker to have fallen in only 15 M.P.H. winds. I don't think he was in good health. He had just had an aneurysm repaired, and I don't think he had his usual strength. When the wind started tossing him around up there on the wire, I think he just gave up; he quit fighting. I know people don't want to hear that, but it's how I feel. Helen especially gets furious with me when I say that."

Whatever went wrong, Karl's words echoed around the

world: "I want to have control over a situation. If I die, I want it to be my fault. The wire is the only place I feel alive. . . . Always the show must go on."

Karl's death impacted all the surviving Wallendas and left them with a maze of confusion and sorrow. It also left them a legacy of courage and fortitude.

For Delilah her only solace was to follow her grandfather's philosophy that the show must go on. After she recuperated, Terry wrote Dave, the family friend who had left the troupe for Bible school, to suggest that he join them to form their own act. They did just that, and within a short time the trio was doing small gigs at one place and another.

But without Vati their financial straits grew more and more dire. "We had to tell Mutti Helen that we could no longer make payments on the trailer Vati had bought for us, so Helen took the trailer back and sold it. We also sold our pick-up because we just couldn't afford it. Dave helped us buy rigging. In addition, my brother lent us some rigging so we could do some dates. Because we didn't have a trailer then," Delilah continues, "we knew we had to rent a U-Haul to put the equipment in and then tow it with our van from one site to another."

Finally their first job came in—a bank opening. To do it, they had to borrow Tino's rig. It took a long time for them to accumulate enough money to purchase their own truck and equipment, and they only did so through scrimping and saving.

Then when Terry and Delilah were on their way back from an engagement, their little daughter Lijana took ill. In the middle of the night, Terry and Delilah got dressed and took her to an area hospital where they learned that she had a nasty ear infection. More bills mounted up.

In May, Delilah discovered she was pregnant again, a child Vati would never see. Delilah realized once again that his death not only left an emptiness inside her, but a cavity in the family as well, and this cavity widened when the surviving Wallendas ended up bickering among themselves.

"I don't know where all the jealously and animosity came from," says Delilah sadly. "I do know that at about that time, Mutti Helen supposedly told Ricky that he could take over Vati's wire act, and I think it all went to his head. He wanted to be Karl Wallenda Jr. or Karl Wallenda reincarnated. He started to deny me the right to the Wallenda name, using everything in his power to prevent me from claiming my Wallenda roots."

Delilah adds, "Nothing has been the same since Vati died. Our family is split and everyone's angry at each other. In fact, right after Vati died, when my mother flew to San Juan with Aunt Carla, Helen acted happy to see Aunt Carla but said to Jenny, 'What are you doing here?' And yet it was my mom who ended up handling all the flight arrangements for Carla, Helen, and the casket," says Delilah.

According to Delilah, Helen's animosity toward Jenny continued. In the cemetery where Vati was laid to rest, were many other circus performers, including Jenny's husband Dick and Martha's nephew Dieter. According to Jenny, Helen, on seeing the plots near Karl's, said to Jenny, "What's your husband doing in my cemetery?"

"I bought the plot from you," replied Jenny. "You never *gave* it to me!"

Jenny clarifies: "I think my sister's family resents mine. I remember when my father died, Helen was talked into holding an auction, and she sold everything, most of it at little cost. As Karl's daughter, you would think I would have been asked how I felt about the auction . . . but I wasn't. The most I got out of it was my father's old leopard chair, which is of no monetary value but has sentimental value to me. My nephew took the photo scrapbook of all the Wallenda performances from Helen's house, and not only haven't I seen it again but I never even got a picture as a memento." Jenny shakes her head sadly. "My father once told me that if anything happened to him that Carla and I wouldn't get anything but our children would. Yet when he died and it came time for the reading of the will, Tino and Delilah weren't even mentioned in it, but all of Carla's kids were. Even my brother Mario only got $5,000 . . . and he's Karl and Helen's son."

Though Delilah worried about her mother being hurt by the internal strife, she forced herself not to dwell on it, but to concentrate on being a good mother as well as proving she was a good performer. She did one more date in New York as an opening act for Fleetwood Mac.

Then, five months into her pregnancy, she stopped working the highwire so that she could rest. She hoped she wouldn't miscarry again.

FIFTEEN

Auspicious Signs

In the weeks to follow, still sorrowing over her beloved grandfather's death while contending with her pregnancy, Delilah tried to sort out her thoughts as to what to do about work. With Karl's death came the death of the wirewalking Wallendas as the world knew them. Delilah could no longer count on acquiring work from a grandfather who once served as the family patriarch and a source of income for all the Wallendas. Not only was her future livelihood threatened, but she couldn't help feeling bitterness over Vati's death, a death she believed should never have happened, a death that was preventable.

She was unable to put his fall out of her mind; she kept envisioning Vati on the wire, slowly trying to get to his knees for balance and then falling. She saw him over and over again in her mind, slamming into a taxi roof and bouncing out onto the ground. *Why did it ever happen?* she continuously asked herself.

Not only was Delilah tormented by the scene of Vati's death, but she felt depressed because the death continued to bring out an enormous amount of jealousy within the family.

Everyone seemed to claim the right to be Karl's designated heir, some going so far as professing to be the *only* heir. Vati's death and the resulting dissension had changed the formerly close-knit Wallenda clan forever. Sometimes Delilah and Terry wondered if they should just quit show business and find "regular" jobs to work. But they loved performing, so they tried to dismiss this dismal thought from their minds and concentrated on happier things as a new year and new baby came into view.

On January 24, 1979, Nikolas came bounding into the world. "He was late, two weeks late," says Delilah. "So the doctor said we had to set a date to induce labor; Terry and I chose the 24th. Five hours after induced labor, he was born —and he looked purple to me."

They laughed that he signaled the future and was "a space baby."

While Delilah recovered from the birth and financial pressures mounted, Terry and Dave continued working in Sarasota while building up their rigging and practicing in the evening. Then to their surprise a contract came in from Circus Vargas—a well-known circus corporation. They were about to rejoice when they noticed the date was a year away; they wondered what they were to do until then. Adding to their worry was the increasing tension building up in the Wallenda family: the troupe had dispersed and everyone was striking out on their own, trying to get the few jobs there were available. The competitive tenor among her relatives dismayed Delilah, but she hoped it was a passing thing.

Meanwhile, Terry and Delilah tried desperately to get bookings. Finally one came in around March, a few months after Nikolas was born. Tino hired his sister to work in Circus Maranatha, where he was doing a date for "The PTL Club" in South Carolina. There, Terry and Dave clowned in the show while Delilah performed the Spanish Web.

One night Delilah sat nursing Nikolas, who was then four months old, when Circus Vargas called again. "We want you to come now. Something's happened to our highwire act."

"Look," she told Mr. Vargas. "We don't have a trailer, we don't have anything right now. We just can't come."

"I'll help you get your truck and trailer. I need you now!"

The Troffers prayed on it with Dave and decided to go. The entire week, they ran around trying to find a truck to buy. However, just as they were about to sign bank loan papers on it, they got a call from Dave, who said, "I don't feel good anymore about doing Vargas. Something inside me has made me change my mind. How about if I come over and with our pastor we pray on it some more?"

They did just that. Their minister read Ecclesiastes 4:12: "If one can over power him who is alone, two can resist him. A cord of three strands is not quickly torn apart."

"We're okay with this, Dave," Terry said after hearing the scripture reading. Dave still felt uncertain, however, so Terry finally called Mr. Vargas, explaining that they couldn't do the performance. Turning to Delilah while hanging up the phone, Terry said, "I figure Vargas will never ask us again to work for him."

However, Vargas still wanted them to do the performance the following year; so the Troffers remained in Sarasota practicing and praying that they would be able to make do until then. As if in answer to their prayers, Gerald Baker, an old friend, called and offered to lend them $2,000 to buy the rest of the rigging. Now they only needed a truck and trailer, and then they'd be set.

They scrimped and saved, taking every job that came along until they were finally able to make a down payment on a truck. Terry and Dave rebuilt the inside for carrying rigging, and Dave finished it off so he could live in it. Delilah and Terry continued looking for a reasonably priced trailer. Word came to them that Mutti Helen was selling the one she and Vati had owned.

"We could really use the trailer," the Troffers told Mutti Helen.

"Okay, I'll sell it to you for $5,000," she proposed.

An agreement was struck so that they could pay it out in installments.

Terry, Delilah, and Dave spent the rest of the year fixing up the trailer and enjoying the holidays, because the day after Christmas they'd be on the road traveling to California to do Circus Vargas.

As the year ended, Delilah felt happy. Her little family was together and there was the promise of work.

In the beginning, Circus Vargas was wonderful. For the first time since Vati's death, the Troffers had employment, security, and some stability. They stayed in one spot for three or four days before having to tear down and start over. As time went on, however, the schedule got more hectic. They had many one-night performances with long driving times in between. To Delilah, it seemed like every second they were driving, setting up, and then tearing down again. Every place the show opened, she had to do two shows daily plus all those interviews and promotions, as well as take care of her children. The stress built up, and pretty soon little disagreements began to come between the Troffers and Dave. Even Terry and Delilah began to get on each other's nerves.

They told themselves they were building a name for themselves, becoming expert performers as independent contractors. But while those positives occurred, they seemed to be more than balanced by unpleasant experiences: they lived through a bomb scare while on the wire, walked the wire with food poisoning, and performed in inclement weather.

Almost as bad as the hectic schedule was, so was the show's deportment. Delilah badly missed the camaraderie of the Wallenda troupe and detested the behavior of some of the workers, who constantly bickered among themselves. Delilah felt overcome with depression, thinking that the situation couldn't possibly turn worse.

And then Terry got ill.

One morning, he woke up with a tremendous headache, so severe he could barely hold his head up.

Later in the day, Delilah suggested, "Let's go to a matinee movie. It might relax you. We've been working so hard that maybe a change in scenery might help, especially if it's a tension headache."

Hoping for some relief, Terry agreed, but no sooner were they seated and the movie had begun, then Terry said, "Delilah, we have to go home, I feel awful."

After resting, Terry felt slightly better.

Hours later, Delilah got ready for the early show she, Terry, and Dave were scheduled to do. Suddenly she noticed that although Terry was getting dressed, too, he looked dazed.

"You can't perform," Delilah told him. "Go to bed."

He did, but the next day he felt worse. On seeing Terry, the circus announcer told him, "You can't work like that."

Delilah took his arm, "Come on, darling, we're going to get you some help." So the Troffers headed for the hospital.

"I think you have meningitis, Mr. Troffer, but I won't know for sure until we do a spinal tap," said the emergency room doctor.

"No," Terry replied flatly.

The doctor shook his head, handed Terry some pain killers and sent him home.

Early the next morning, Terry's head was pounding so forcefully that he said to Delilah, "All I want to do is curl up and die." Delilah rushed him back to the hospital, where a different doctor told him, "You have some kind of viral infection. Take this medication and go to bed."

Terry obeyed while Delilah went off to perform. When he woke up hours later, Delilah took one look at him and said, "You're still sick."

"I'm alright," Terry objected. They packed up and left. But once they were on the road he worsened, and Delilah rushed him to still another hospital, where the physician confirmed the first doctor's diagnosis: "I think it's meningitis," he said soberly. "We need a spinal tap to be sure."

"I don't want it." Terry replied. "We're traveling far from home and we have no family around. I'll wait until I get back to Sarasota."

"Then see a specialist . . . a neurosurgeon," countered the doctor. "You need medical care. And I think the medicine that second doctor gave you for a supposed virus only aggravated the meningitis."

Somehow Terry convinced Delilah they could make it home, and once again they left town. Deleilah insisted on driving, and on the road Terry slept all day and night. In the next town Delilah told her husband, "I'm not listening to you anymore." She called a neurosurgeon, who put Terry in the hospital with the explicit intention of doing a spinal tap. Miraculously, Terry began showing signs of improvement and insisted on leaving the hospital. The doctor asked, "What town are you going to next?" He gave Terry the name of a specialist there. Delilah was determined to take Terry to see him.

However, when the Troffers got there, Terry told Delilah,

"You know, I do feel better, so I don't need to see a specialist . . . except that I feel drunk on one side of my brain."

Delilah smiled at the image, knowing her husband was at least getting better. Still, she took him to another doctor.

"I won't commit myself to a diagnosis," said this physician, "but I think it's either meningitis or encephalitis. Whatever it is, though, I can tell it's subsiding."

Terry and Delilah asked their church friends to pray for Terry. With the help of prayer, Terry's healing continued, and one week later he returned to performing.

In 1981 the Troffers learned Dave was getting married and leaving the act. Because Terry and Delilah had invested so much time in working with him, they suggested, "We'll wait until you and your new wife settle in before we go back on the road."

Dave shook his head. "I don't want that anymore; I don't even want to work the wire. I just wanna get married, stay home, and be a family man."

For some reason Terry was dubious, then he asked Dave point-blank, "Are you leaving us to work for Ricky?"

Dave replied, "Of course not; I just want to get out of this crazy business."

Finally the Troffers accepted his decision. They paid Dave what their accountant said was fair, taking into consideration that Dave had used the truck for his living quarters for a year. A disagreement resulted, and with that, Dave and the Troffers parted on unfriendly terms. Delilah and Terry had to hire someone else for the act.

They came across Mike, a tall, blond young man, who seemed like a nice guy and who willingly moved to Sarasota to join the Troffers after New Year's. The three started practicing. After a short time, Mike began, smoothly going from walking the wire at two feet to ten. Of course, Terry and Delilah still missed Dave and were further hurt when word came that Dave and his new bride had gone to work for Ricky.

A couple of months later, Terry, Delilah, and Mike opened in Montreal, and although Mike was a little shaky on the wire at thirty feet, the Troffers didn't worry; they knew it took time to get adjusted to performing at that height. Six days later, even after doing three shows a day, Mike was still weak on the wire . . . but strong in the women department. Delilah comments, "Mike's blond like Terry, and the girls went nuts over him. I guess in Montreal they like blonds."

Still, jobs were scarce. About this time, to acquire more bookings, Terry had a photographer take expensive colored publicity photos of the three of them to send to promoters. The trio then headed for Los Angeles, where Mike approached Terry before the first show started and demanded, "You want me to walk the wire? I want more money."

"Pack your bags and go," responded Terry.

Mike quickly changed his mind and returned to practicing. The three had a month off before working at Sea World in San Diego, so they stayed in Los Angeles near a friend and set up their rigging in his backyard for practice. The three rehearsed every day and then left for Sea World a week early. Everything was set.

At Sea World Delilah and the trio, who didn't want to escalate the bad feeling on the part of the other Wallendas about who should use the name, billed themselves as "The Zaltanas." The children and Delilah went on a promotional tour for the company, which even sent along a nanny to take care of the children while Delilah was on the road for eight days in Salt Lake City, Las Vegas, and other places. Meanwhile, Terry and Mike were busy setting up the rigging at

Sea World, where they were given a nice dressing room in a beautiful, well-kept park. When the performances began, the schedule was hectic. They did four shows a day, six days a week, with one day off. Their repertoire consisted of five acts, which they alternated.

While in Sea World, much publicity was done on Terry and Delilah. In one piece in particular, featured in *Currents* magazine, Delilah reflected on her life:

> Four times a day Delilah Troffer climbs 30 feet above the ring beside Mission Bay to perform gasp-evoking high-wire stunts of amazing grace and balance with her husband, Terry. . . . "I really don't remember when I started," she said. "But I didn't begin to perform pro- fessionally until I was 18 or 19. My parents wanted me to graduate from high school. . . . My grandfather taught me . . . gave me little tips, but never encour- aged me to do any tricks." Delilah remembers that the first time her grandfather saw her do the stunt [the "backward revolve"], he gasped and shouted, "You learn that behind my back!" She was 19 when he al- lowed her to work with his act. "He didn't suggest that I do any tricks," she said. "He thought I was just some- thing to look pretty and talk to." She had been working with him for eight years when on March 21, 1978, he went to San Juan. . . .[31]

The promo piece brought Delilah much acclaim but also angered some of the Wallendas who didn't like Delilah "walking in her grandfather's footsteps," as the reporter had observed a the end of the article.

Says Delilah, "It was while we were performing in San Diego with Mike, our new man, that we got word of a letter addressed to Sea World personnel. It was from a Florida law office, dated August 11th. I remember it well."

Gentlemen:

I represent Mrs. Helen Wallenda, the wife of the late famous aerial, Karl Wallenda. Mrs. Wallenda has recently become aware that Terry and Delilah Troffer have been performing at Sea World and using the name "The Flying Wallendas." . . . Their use of the Wallenda name is not authorized and any participation on your part is wrongful.

Angry about the letter, and sensing that it boded unwarranted trouble, Sea World's entertainment director wrote back that Terry and Delilah had not misrepresented themselves and that they were using the name Zaltanas.

Ricky had teamed up with his half-sister Rietta and two other friends to form a group billed as the "The Great Wallendas." Dispirited, Delilah wondered why he could use the name when, according to the lawyer's letter, she herself was prohibited. Delilah seethed.

To add to the Troffers' worries, at about the same time, Mike went over to the Sea World office and told a clerk, "I need to see the Wallenda contract." The clerk handed it to him. Mike read it, whistled, returned the contract to the files. Then he sought out Terry and demanded a raise, saying if they make that much money, he deserved to make more, too. "But Mike had no understanding of our overhead and other expenses," says Delilah. "His only cost was to pay for his food. We had a truck, trailer, rigging, other overhead costs, and a wardrobe to take care of, not counting other things such as public relations expenses. For example, those earlier publicity photos we had taken of the three of us and things like that cost a lot of money. With Mike a little irritated with us for denying him a raise, we closed up in Sea World on Labor Day and headed home." Although the park apologized to the Troffers for allowing an unauthorized person to see their contract, it did not change the fact that after this Mike was under the misconception that Delilah and Terry were rolling in money.

At home in Sarasota, Delilah learned that Showfolks—the organization her grandfather had belonged to—had gotten hold of the balancing pole he used in the San Juan walk and cut it into one-inch pieces, which they mounted in plastic and sold for about $17.50 each as a fund raiser. She told Terry, "It's a good idea; Showfolks is an organization that wouldn't exploit Vati, they'll put that money to good use. My Grandfather would have liked that."

Within days Terry returned to working for his father, Delilah occupied herself with the children, and Mike obtained a job as an orderly at a nursing home while living in his trailer on the Troffers' lot. Their evenings were devoted to practicing on the wire, and when he was not rehearsing, Terry was busy promoting the trio. Things weren't easy, but the Troffers tried to be optimistic. Still, they could see that something was eating at Mike.

Around the middle of October, Mike crossed the lawn, knocked on the Troffers' door, and issued another ultimatum—he wanted one-third of the trio's gross income or he would quit. Terry shook his head, saying, "Look, I think you'd better go." And that was the end of Mike. Delilah and Terry started to practice a two-person act, billing themselves, "The Delilah Wallenda Duo."

"It was a terrible time," says Delilah. "We sat at home after that for quite a while without work."

A little later a friend told them that, like Dave, Mike went to work for Ricky.

And so 1981 was ushered out. Just as the economy of America was on the skids, so were the Troffers. They were unemployed for a total of eight months.

*   *   *

In early January, Delilah legally changed her name from Delilah Zaira Diana Troffer to Delilah Wallenda Troffer in hopes of cementing her heritage and helping her career. Almost simultaneously, Delilah and Terry got booked in Atlanta. They thought it a good sign, but then Delilah came down with a bad case of the jitters. This was really to be her first time working alone; she'd always been in a troupe, or at least a trio. But after a few performances, when the audiences loved her, she gained more confidence. From then the Troffers joined Tino at Circus Maranatha. Before they knew it, the job was done and they were back on the road home. There they waited for the phone to ring. At last a June two-week date came in for Camden Park in Huntington, West Virginia.

When they got there, to their shock, they saw the wording "The Great Wallendas" on the giant marquis outside the park.

"It's the wrong billing," Delilah told the park director. "We're called the Delilah Wallenda Duo, not the Great Wallendas. You have to change it."

And it did get changed—immediately. A few days later, however, Delilah got called back to the office, where she was asked, "Who's Helen Wallenda?"

"Why?"

"She just called and yelled on the phone, saying you're *not* a Wallenda at all."

"Well let me tell you . . . ," began Delilah, who quickly straightened them out.

Shortly after her West Virginia engagement, Delilah received a letter from the Camden Point Circus director stating: "We were delighted with your act and wish to apologize for any inconveniences we may have caused inadvertently with our advertising . . . [but] as far as Camden park is concerned, you two *are* great.''

From Camden Park the Troffers went back for the fourth time to the PTL Club's Circus Maranatha to do more work for Tino. Then they were off to Canobie Lake Park in Salem, New Hampshire, for two weeks. Here they were made to feel right at home. Everything about the park seemed right; more importantly, they were glad to be in the same place for a few weeks. They set up their equipment and settled in. A few days later, they drove with their children to the nearest mall to meet Terry's parents. Afterward, Mr. and Mrs. Troffer went on their way vacationing to other spots, and Terry and Delilah announced to their kids, "Let's get pizza." They stopped at a little shopping center.

"I need to pick up a few items at the grocery store first," Delilah said. They purchased more than they intended. "We better put these in the truck," Delilah said, weighted down. So she, Terry, and the kids made a dash through the rain, which had started to fall, toward their vehicle carrying the bags. When they got to the spot where they had parked their truck, the truck was nowhere to be seen. Dumfounded, they stood around staring at each other. "We'd better scout around the parking lot, maybe we left it elsewhere," Terry said. But the truck was nowhere in sight.

"It's been stolen," Delilah finally decreed, her mouth open, eyes mirroring shock. "All the wardrobe costumes were inside it."

The first thing they did was pray, and then they called the police, who agreed to drive out and take down all the necessary information.

Finishing up their questioning, one officer remarked, "I hate to tell you this, but you'll never get your truck back."

Delilah shrugged. "It belongs to God, and if we don't get it back we'll end up with something better."

In the meantime, Terry's parents talked to their daughter —whom Terry had called—and learned about the stolen truck. They broke off their vacation early and traveled to Canobie to see if they could help in any way.

The truck was at last found near Boston, about 50 miles from where the Troffers had parked it. It had been taken to some Boston suburb that Terry tried to locate on a map, while suggesting, "Let's first do the three shows we're scheduled for today, and then go off to hunt for the town."

Delilah agreed and began to get ready for their first show. She ran right into a spectator. "Your act was wonderful," the tall, balding man said.

"I really appreciate hearing that," she told him. "We've been a little distracted since someone stole our truck. And now we have to find the place where they keep the recovered cars."

"My name is Tom Beauford, and I had a car swiped, too, so I know what that's like." He paused a moment, then generously offered, "Hey, I know where they take the vehicles after they've been found. . . . Would you like me to show you?"

"That is really nice of you, Tom."

Graciously and gratefully the Troffers accepted his offer. Beauford patiently waited for them to finish their performances.

The truck was right where he thought it would be, but while their wardrobe was there, a lot of their things were gone. Terry's tools were missing, along with his guitar, two leather coats, even their washing machine, and many other items—all amounting to about $5,000, with their insurance covering only $500 worth of it.

As Delilah and Terry sifted thought the topsy-turvied

truck, Beauford stood to the side, watching, helpless to do anything more. He glanced at an item sitting untouched on an end table and said, "Look! At least they didn't steal your Bible."

"It's the one thing I wanted them to take," said Terry quietly.

As time passed, the Troffers worked hard and gradually replaced the stolen items. In March 1983, Terry and Delilah worked for Tripoli Temple, still performing as the Delilah Wallenda Duo. Another letter arrived addressed to the circus chairman on behalf of Helen Wallenda, and again it dealt with the Wallenda name.

Terry and Delilah's attorney responded by sending a letter to Helen's attorney:

> On several occasions you have written letters to organizations who have employed the Troffers to do a high-wire act. . . . As I indicated to you on the telephone, Delilah Troffer changed her name legally on January 18, 1982. . . . As I also told you, the Troffers have billed themselves as the "Delilah Wallenda Duo." At no time have they ever had themselves billed out as "The Flying Wallendas" or "The Great Wallendas." In fact, they have gone out of their way to make certain no one mistakes their act as being in any way related to the latter two names in quotations. Please advise your clients that their continued harassment of my clients by contacting their employers and making allegations about unauthorized name usage will not be tolerated any longer. In fact, if such wrongful accusations result in my clients losing a job, then such legal action for damages may

ensue. I trust it will not be necessary to pursue this matter any further.

However, Helen obviously was not content, since she had her attorney issue another letter dated April 4th, stating that she wanted Delilah to use the title of "Delilah Wallenda and Partner" because she objected to Terry billing himself as a Wallenda.

Again the Troffers' attorney replied:

> I do not believe that this is an acceptable alternative and the Troffers agree. . . . There are numerous situations in which entertainment groups are designated by a lead performer or entertainer, such as the Dave Brubeck Quartet. In that situation, I don't believe anyone would be under the impression that all members Mr. Brubeck's quartet are his brothers or are named Brubeck.

No response came to this letter, and Terry and Delilah went on rightfully using the Wallenda name. Although discouraged, they attempted to carry on with their lives, and accepted a six-week run with a small show, Hetzer Circus. In the show Delilah performed the "cloud swing" because it required less rigging; in the summer, she and Terry planned to return to their world famous wirewalks. Of course, at Hetzer the money wasn't as good as they'd gotten for the wire, but at least they had their trailer paid off and only a year left to pay on the truck. So they felt they were making some headway.

They even started thinking about building a house.

"We can save money if we act as our own contractors," Terry interjected. Delilah's eyes were shining.

"It would be heaven to have our own place."

They began planning the house, but the paperwork took so long that they were back on the road and no longer around to do the work. John Wordman, a friend who was a builder, stepped in, saying, "I'll act as the subcontractor for you while you're on the road."

The year 1984 marked eight years of marriage for the Troffers. On their anniversary they broke ground for their first home. The Troffer family was excited and couldn't wait to see their house constructed. "I want to see every brick set," Delilah told Terry, "that is, if I can't do it myself."

Terry smiled, "There are some things better left to professionals. Remember the time you decided to fix your mother's roof?"

The memory of the early days of their love made them nostalgic. They laughed and hugged each other. "Anyway, Delilah," Terry said, more serious now, "if we're going to pay for all this we'd better go back on the road."

And they did.

First, it was back to doing the cloud swing in March, then they moved on to parks and fairs in the summer, then to another circus in the fall. In the meanwhile they paid off their truck, and things really started to look better.

Best of all, by October, it was time to go home.

Delilah and the children sat in the truck, their noses pressed to the windows as they drove down their street, wondering what their new home would look like.

Says Delilah, "I remember it was October, and as Terry drove down our street, I was noticing, as if for the first time, all the houses and how beautiful everything looked. And then I saw our new house. I was breathless! I just couldn't believe it. It looked regal and stately, much more beautiful than I had ever imagined—and it's only a ranch. But it was *our* home, not some trailer or camper, but a real home."

They spent their first night sleeping on the floor of their new castle since they didn't have beds yet. The discomfort did not matter. They thought it one of the best times in their lives.

Soon Terry was back to working the winter months for his father while Delilah stayed home and took care of the family. Already they had a summer booking for a park in New Hampshire. Everything seemed to be perfect. That was what worried her.

SIXTEEN

Ups and Downs

Like the world's bipolar swings, Delilah noticed her life always oscillated from one extreme to another. Sometimes things seemed even and flowing, while other times they were clogged and inequitable.

The year 1985 began with a death—that of Herman Wallenda, Karl's older brother, who was 83. Born in Grossottersleben, Germany, he had moved with Karl to Sarasota in 1928. Herman's obituary called him "the last male family member of the original Wallendas." His death brought sadness to the remaining members of the family, but it was a merciful death at the end of a long and fruitful life. That in itself comforted the mourners—that it was not a death like Vati's, where he thudded onto the roof of a taxi. Delilah shuddered at the thought.

Already Delilah was beginning to worry that this year was going to be another lean one. They did have the summer commitment at Benson's Animal Park, for Memorial Day through Labor Day, but this wasn't enough to keep them going and no other booking had come in. The entertainment world was tough, and getting even tougher. Terry, Delilah, and their children struggled to make ends meet, never relaxing, never sure where their next job would come from, how far they would have to travel to get it, and if, in the end, it would be worth it. Life in show business, says Delilah, can be very bitter or very sweet: "There are times when we drive all night, set up the rig, do the shows, tear down, and drive all night again to the next job. But when we're lucky, we get a booking at a park for the summer, and then we only have to set up and tear down once. Those, however, are a rarity."

As difficult as being on the road could be for Terry and Delilah, it was also hard for the children, who were never able to make lasting friends or get involved in sports, band, or other extracurricular activities, or even get a consistent education. By schooling the children at home, Delilah tried to give them the same quality education they would have gotten at school, but she knew it had both benefits and limitations. She taught the same courses and used the same textbooks; however, they didn't have the advantage of other classroom discussions with other children, and that often worried her. Still, in some ways she believed her tutoring turned out to be more beneficial since they had the same teacher—and a loving one at that—all the time, and she was working one-on-one with them. On the other hand, she was more than aware of the disadvantages.

Though Delilah agonized over the quality of her children's education, both she and Terry considered it a blessing having their children with them all the time. "In normal circumstances, the kids leave the parents in the morning and return late in the afternoon, so the parents don't see their children all day, and thus they don't always know who they're hanging around with or what they're doing—if they're smoking, trying drugs, whatever. But in our case, our children are with us all the time, so we can monitor them. We do know who they loaf around with and what they're up to. Sure, sometimes we get under each other's feet, but still we're more secure knowing our children are safe with us," says Delilah. "We spend a lot of quality time together. And we do get to play with them, just kind of goof around sometimes, and that's nice. We're a tight, solid family."

The children live normal lives when bookings don't come in for their parents; then their father works for his father, and their mother stays home or helps out in her father-in-law's business. "So really we're not much different than the average American, except that we prefer to walk on air while the rest of the world walks on the ground," says Delilah.

It is a preference which didn't find expression in January or February of that year. Delilah and Terry found no circus work.

Finally, in March, a call came in from Clyde Beatty. A hired act couldn't leave Canada because of paperwork problems, so the Troffers were asked to substitute for a few weeks. Elated at the opportunity, Terry said sure and named his price. Clyde Beatty replied that he'd get back to them before the week was up. Days passed and still there was no word from Beatty. They started worrying that they had asked too much. "Don't pack or prepare the trailer," Terry discouragingly told Delilah. "If Beatty hasn't called by now, he's not going to."

Delilah injects, "Then around 10:00 P.M., the night before Clyde Beatty was to open, we get a call from them saying they want us to do the two weeks. Terry and I and the children hugged each other. I spent all night packing and getting ready so we could leave the first thing in the morning to drive the 200 or 300 miles in Florida to the site. We arrived just in time to set up."

The act went well. The Troffers were pleased and so, it seemed, was everyone else.

Nearly a week later, however, an old man approached Terry and told him, "I'm an ex-wirewalker who was in direct competition with Karl Wallenda. I can't begin to tell you how much I hated him." On and on the man went, denigrating Karl and his family.

Terry held his tongue, deferring to the raving old man. But when the man started demeaning Delilah's grandmother Martha, Terry forgot respect and told him, "Stop bad-mouthing Delilah's family or just don't bother to talk with us!"

The next day the Troffers climbed the platform to do a show. They spotted cigarette butts and ashes all around, and though disgusted, they went on with the performance. Then it was time for their bicycle stunt. As usual, Terry pedaled to the middle of the wire, stood on the pedals, lifted his pole over his head, and began to go into this routine. Suddenly a pedal snapped off.

Delilah gasped. Her husband was about to plummet to the ground 30 feet below them. She motioned that she'd wirewalk out to help him.

Terry pantomimed back that he couldn't make out what she was saying. On a prayer, he managed to return to the platform, pedaling in on one pedal and looking shaken. Later, Delilah said to him, "It should have never happened. Something's wrong. You check the equipment all the time, especially the bike. In all the years we've done that routine, it's never happened."

Terry looked at her. "Are you thinking the same thing?"

Delilah nodded. "That the old man sabotaged our act?"

Immediately the Troffers started searching for Karl's former competitor, but says Delilah, "Somehow he had magically disappeared with no one knowing how he came or where he went." Terry and Delilah went back to focusing on the Beatty run.

At the end of their time with the Beatty circus, the Troffers were asked to renew their contract, but although they'd been without work all year, they did have that Memorial Day commitment with Benson's Animal Park and after that they had been invited to compete in England for the Circus Championship contest. They had to decline Beatty's offer.

A few days later, on their way to Benson's, Terry and Delilah realized their old truck was still acting up, so they tossed around the idea of buying a new one. "Without a vehicle," said Terry, "we can't make it from one site to another, and hence can't work." They immediately started looking for reliable transportation.

Luckily, while at Benson's they found a truck at a dealership, and by the time they closed at the park, they were on their way to Indiana to pick up their new possession. They did a one-day engagement along the way, and then headed back home to Sarasota to attend Terry's sister's wedding. The next day, leaving Nikolas and Lijana with Mr. and Mrs. Troffer, they headed for England, where they were competing in the Circus Championships—a major international contest. To their delight, they won second place in their category. Collecting their trophy, they hoped that this would make them better known around the world. Then they were on their way home to settle in for the winter.

Perhaps it was the contest or just good luck for a change, but May 1986 ushered in Delilah's big moment—a moment performers wait for. It happened while she and Terry were booked with Circus Flora in Charleston, South Carolina. A coastal community of about 70,000 people, Charleston was holding its annual gala event—the Spoleto Festival U.S.A. Noted personalities from around the world were scheduled to attend, and some of the world's best entertainment was to be featured.

Delilah and Terry were aware of Spoleto's activities across the street as it readied for opening day, but they were too busy setting up with Circus Flora to pay it much attention. Terry was having trouble getting the rigging inside Flora's tent, so he had to call a welder. Mumbling when the welder was late, Terry tried setting up the rigging himself when Delilah walked over to him.

"I heard a rumor that Spoleto's interested in my doing a skywalk . . . can you believe it? A skywalk!" Delilah said excitedly.

Terry looked at her. "But there's nothing official?"

Delilah shook her head.

Terry returned to fighting with the rigging. How would she do it anyway? he wondered. They had no equipment for a skywalk, and she had not even practiced it. He let the matter drop.

The next day a group of strangers approached Delilah.

"We would like you to do a skywalk for Spoleto like your grandfather did. Would you open the festivities with one?" they asked.

Delilah's eyes widened. She thought, *They're asking me!* Instantly she understood: They heard the name Wallenda, made the connection, and automatically thought that she too was as versed as Vati had been, as though walking the highwire was something she did by the nature of her genes. She nodded enthusiastically, neglecting to add that she had never walked at great heights before. The highwire wasn't the same as a skywalk, which required stringing a cable between rooftops of tall buildings. When Vati was alive, Delilah had nagged him about wanting to do skywalks, but he

225

would just shrug and say, "In time, in time. Your moment will come."

Standing there, Delilah realized that this was her moment. And although she was eager to at last demonstrate her highwire prowess, she knew the logistics had to be worked out.

As soon as the strangers left, she sought out Terry and told him the news.

"Do you want to?" he asked. "I don't want you pressured into doing something that you're not ready for. It's so dangerous." His eyes were filled with love. "But if you really want to, there's no doubt in my mind that you can do it."

"This is my life's dream. Now is my time. I should take advantage of it."

Terry nodded his assent.

Later that day, Delilah called her mother to tell her about it.

"I don't think you should do it," Jenny countered. "The whole thing's been arranged too quickly. And what will you do for the wire? You'll end up having to borrow a cable from a Navy yard, and that will be too slick because of the grease on it."

Delilah understood that her mother's mind must be filled with pictures of Vati falling when he, too, had hastily agreed to do a skywalk. After the call Delilah sought out Terry, who was standing outside, leaning against the tent. Running up to him she told him quickly what her mother had said. Then she looked at him more closely, "What's wrong? Why are you rubbing your eye so much?"

"I don't know, but it hurts a lot and gets awfully blurry."

"Maybe you've got something in it," Delilah said concerned.

"No, it will be alright," Terry replied, but when it became agonizing, Delilah realized he needed to see a doctor. She tried to get him an appointment with an eye specialist between meetings with Spoleto officials. A few mornings later, while talking with the mayor, Delilah saw Terry looking pale and miserable and rubbing his eye again. He was explaining, "You understand, Mr. Mayor, we're committed to Circus Flora and are trying to set up for that—" Then Terry stopped and covered his throbbing eye with his hand.

Realizing Terry was in pain, the mayor asked him what was wrong. Hearing that Terry couldn't get in to see an eye specialist, the mayor picked up the phone, dialed a number, then turned back to Terry and said, "I've made arrangements for a leading opthamologist to see you in the morning. Now about this skywalk . . ." He turned to Delilah, who still hadn't made a decision, and told her, "I'll call for an answer in the next few days."

After leaving, Terry and Delilah discussed another aspect about the skywalk, "What should we charge?" she asked. She and Terry talked about the fee, and then agreed on a price.

"They won't go for it," said Terry. "They'll say they can't meet our price."

Delilah shook her head. "When you risk your life for the pleasure of others, you have to be well paid."

The next day Terry went to the eye doctor appointment the mayor had made. While waiting, he was told he was wanted on the phone. "Terry," began the mayor, "I'm sending a car over to pick you up when you're finished there. We need to finalize these arrangements. Opening day is tomorrow."

Terry agreed, wishing he could leave the doctor's office. However, the doctor walked in, looked into Terry's eyes, studied them some more, and then called his associate over.

At last Terry asked, "Do you see anything?"

"Yes," said one of the specialists. "But we don't know what it is. You're going to have to see a cornea specialist."

The doctors' receptionist called the local university eye clinic to set up an appointment. Her face grimaced and turned to Terry and said, "They're booked; you'll have to go on a three-month waiting list."

"You don't understand; my wife and I will be in Charleston for only three days. I can't wait that long anyway; the pain really is bad. And what if my eye gets worse while I'm waiting?" Terry left the office knowing he had to find a specialist immediately. The second he was outside, he saw the mayor's car waiting for him.

In the mayor's office, part of the committee waited; the skywalk was deliberated some more. "What's your price?" asked the mayor.

"We've already told them," Terry said naming it.

"Bottom line?"

Terry nodded.

"Just a minute." He and his entourage left the office for a second and returned. "Okay, let's do it. The festival starts tomorrow morning, and your wife is to be the opening act. We need to hustle."

Though his eye was badly aching, Terry planned the construction of the skywalk. "Here's what we need for Delilah to walk the wire," Terry said.

"Don't worry, we'll get it," they replied, and went as far as offering to send a jet to get whatever else was needed.

Terry laughed. "I don't think that will be necessary. Why don't you borrow what's needed; it's quicker and cheaper." The committee agreed.

Terry emphasized, "You people are going to be the ones to erect the skywalk, because Delilah and I are under contract with Circus Flora and can't leave the act."

The committee looked nervously from one to the other, but in no time they had the construction underway. With Terry's direction, they had workers drag the cable through dirt in order to get the grease off. Engineers checked the buildings to make sure they were strong enough to hold both the cable and Delilah and to reinforce areas where crewmen had attached guy wires.

Like Terry, Delilah was busy. She had to prepare for her first skywalk, one she would have to do based strictly on her husband's verbal direction since she did not have hands-on experience. As she tried to get comfortable with this, the Troffers were still having trouble customizing their rigging to fit into Circus Flora's tent. All this, and especially seeing her husband in pain, worried her. But she knew she had to keep her mind focused strictly on the performance if she was to succeed.

On the morning of Spoleto's opening ceremonies, Terry woke early to meet with an eye specialist, who told him he had a viral keratitis—something similar to the herpes simplex virus. It was a leading cause of corneal lesions and blindness. He gave Terry eye drops which improved the condition enough to give Terry some relief from the pain. Terry returned to his trailer to discuss with Delilah what the doctor had said and then headed over to the site where the skywalk was being constructed. Time was running out.

The opening ceremony was scheduled for 11:00 A.M.; the cable had to be strung between City Hall and the post office, about 200 feet across and 80 feet high. Terry watched the crewman intently.

While Delilah readied for her big moment, one of the ladies on the festival committee took Nikolas and Lijana out on the street to watch their mother. As soon as Delilah was dressed, she left her trailer and went up on the roof where Terry was already waiting. "How's your eye?" she asked.

"Fine. How are you?" he asked.

"Fine, too." She smiled at him. Then Delilah turned her attention to the cable. She ran her glance across it to the other side so she'd know how to exit, remembering Vati having said at Tallulah Gorge, "These catwalks are sometimes the hardest thing to get off." Behind her, Terry murmured, "I'll be going down to the street to run between buildings so I can meet you at the other side and grab your pole when you get there." Delilah nodded, still examining her exit platform, noting that she had to go through the window of the post office in order to get down from the wire.

Suddenly she turned to Terry before he left for the street and asked, "Where's my pole?"

"Don't worry, it's coming."

"I haven't even had time to practice with it," she said frowning.

The mayor had already started his speech just as a worker handed her the pole.

Within minutes Delilah stood on the top floor of City Hall, ready to go through the open window to start her walk. She saw friends below holding the ropes. She felt secure knowing everything was proper and secure, because, after all, it was her husband who had put it together for her.

"And now, ladies and gentlemen," the announcer called out in a deep, sonorous voice, "for an act that's unparalleled anywhere, one that's stunning and dangerous, one carried on in the tradition of world famous Karl Wallenda, Delilah Wallenda will skywalk between two tall buildings."

The crowd screamed.

Delilah turned to Terry, who was ready to charge down the elevator to get out on the street, and said to him, "I love you." Then giving him a kiss, she stepped up on the cable and began the walk.

As she stepped out, her first thought was that the wire felt looser than she was used to. Next she noticed that everything had gone absolutely silent. Even the church bells ceased tolling in mid-chime; someone later told her it was the only time the bells stopped ringing at noon. Since this was her first skywalk, Delilah was prepared to be nervous up there, but she was pleasantly surprised to see she was not. "I was shakier when the pedal snapped off Terry's bike than I was doing my first skywalk," says Delilah.

She was now in the middle of the wire and debating with herself over whether to do a salute or go into a full split. The crowd was pin-drop quiet. She wondered if they were afraid she was going to fall. Delilah looked to the other end of the cable, hoping to catch sight of Terry so that he might through some marital telepathy tell her which stunt to do. But he wasn't there yet. She continued walking. Again she looked across the cable, but still no Terry.

"Then, from the corner of my eyes," says Delilah, "I glimpsed Terry running on the ground underneath the cable to get into the post office building. I thought, 'Gosh, he needs to be at the other end to help me off, and all he's doing is running between buildings like a white flash,'" she adds, laughing.

Okay, she decided, she'd do the split, because it took more time and by then Terry would be there. Other thoughts spun through her mind: *Am I walking too fast? Maybe I ought to slow down. I've only been up here six or seven minutes, and already I'm almost to the end.* Once again she looked around —still no Terry. All right, maybe she wouldn't do the split, but she would slow down and if Terry still wasn't there by the time she got to the end, she'd just have to ask some of the news people waiting at the opposite end to help her climb down through the window. Despite the barrage of thoughts passing through her mind, she began to slowly slide her legs and did the split perfectly. The viewers applauded wildly.

Suddenly Terry appeared in the window frame and smiled at her.

231

She grinned back, tip-toed a few more feet and reached the end of the wire.

Terry reached out, took her pole, helped her down through the window, and gave her a giant hug. Cameras flashed. The man with her paycheck stood there, smiling. He handed it to her.

"Thanks," she said, her feet on solid ground. "You know, I've never done a skywalk before."

He gasped and turned pale.

Then he stuttered, "Had I known that, you wouldn't have done it now either."

She grinned a cheshire cat grin, knowing at last she had gotten a chance to prove herself, and from then on in, she could do any skywalk she wanted. Next she posed for the cameras, took her husband's arm, and together, hand-in-hand, they went off to rejoin their children and celebrate.

Then, as is true now, Delilah Wallenda was the only female world-wide to perform skywalks at such heights.

In the trailer, she told Terry, "I fulfilled my dream . . . I walked in Vati's steps."

That night, she and Terry did their evening performance. She was feeling high, he was feeling better, and everything was wonderful. The next morning, Delilah's picture was splashed all over the newspapers, far and near. Instantly she was a star. Even the mayor was happy. He called and invited the Troffer family to breakfast with him the next day—an honor for everyone in the festival. He told them he had photos made of Delilah's skywalk which he wanted her to autograph.

But the next day, Terry again awakened with his eye throbbing, and unrelenting agony. "I'm too sick to go to the mayor's breakfast, but you and the kids should go. I'll call to see if I can get a doctor's appointment."

Delilah reluctantly agreed and spent what seemed like

hours signing her name on photos and thanking everyone for their wonderful comments. All the while, her worry about her husband mounted. When she returned, Terry was back from seeing the doctor.

"What did he say?" Delilah asked anxiously.

"He told me that the eye drops prescribed by the other doctor are aggravating the condition, causing an infection, so he gave me a different medication to counteract the first one." Wincing, Terry applied the new medicine.

"Terry, the pain you have seems a lot worse than that," Delilah said, watching him. He nodded.

Two days later, Terry was back in the doctor's office; the pain was worse.

This time the doctor told him, "The virus has caused some tissue scarring on your cornea which has to be surgically removed. I'm not charging you for your visits to me, my consultations, or even your surgery, but I want you in the hospital tonight."

Terry thanked him, went home, and packed a few things. Then, with Delilah next to him, he drove to the hospital and checked in.

A few days after the surgery, the doctor advised, "Although this was a nasty case, the odds of your getting the same disease in your other eye is one in a million. You'll be fine now. Use the medication to keep the virus under control, and put drops in your eye, since dust can cause it to act up again. But don't worry. It's over with."

Terry thanked him and returned to Circus Flora for six weeks. Then they performed at a few fairs. With things looking up once again, the Troffers started for home.

Near the end of the year, Delilah received word that her step-grandfather, J.Y., had been in a terrible car accident that put him in the hospital. He stayed there for five weeks. Before discharging him, the doctor cautioned that he would

have to go into a rehabilitation center for a long while. So
J.Y. turned glum and despondent.

Delilah talked to the doctor. "Can you release him into my
care?"

"You're a small woman," said the doctor, "and he's a big
man. There's no way you can take care of him."

Delilah was stubborn. For days she badgered the doctor
until he finally relented. "You'll have to accompany him to
therapy a couple of days a week."

"I'll do whatever he needs," Delilah said resolutely.

The doctor nodded and turned to leave. Just as quickly he
spun around, saying, "By the way, I was at Spoleto and saw
you walk the wire. You were wonderful."

Delilah smiled.

Diligently she cared for J.Y. until she had to go back on
the road. Then his daughter Lelia moved into Delilah's home
to substitute for her. Three months later, Lelia found a house
of her own where she and her father decided to live.

At the end of the year, a photographer approached Delilah
to do a newspaper article featuring her, Lijana, Jenny, and
Helen. The piece would discuss four generations of Wallendas. Helen represented one, Jenny the next, Delilah the
third, and Lijana the fourth.

After the article came out Ricky and Delilah got into another arguement over whether she was claiming to be related to Helen—his blood grandmother. "I wasn't," Delilah
says. "I never claimed that, yet Helen has always wanted me
to consider her as my grandmother—Mutti Helen—especially after my grandmother died."

And so as another year ended, the bickering in the Wallenda family went on.

SEVENTEEN

Echoes and Forecasts

Despite the tension among the now divided Wallendas, 1987 started out fine. "We got a phone call about my doing a skywalk in Puerto Rico," Delilah says, "the same place Vati died. I was determined to do it in honor of him. The promoter, Terry, and I went back and forth about the walk, and then we were invited down, expenses paid, to look at the site and do some advance promos."

When the promoter mentioned something about televising the walk, Delilah turned the discussion over to Terry. Terry told him, "Let me explain something: You can broadcast a clip of Delilah's walk, but you can't televise the entire thing without paying her extra. Besides, why would anyone go in person to watch the walk, fight the crowds, crane their necks, if they could see it on TV in the comfort of their homes?"

"I understand," said the promoter. "There will be no violations." He gave the Troffers a substantial deposit, and everyone signed the contracts for the planned August 16th skywalk. Then the Troffers returned to Florida to try to get more bookings before the walk.

They were glad when one came in for April. They signed on for ten days with Circus-Plus in New Jersey.[32] Here they returned to their two-person act. So pleased was Circus-Plus with the Delilah Wallenda Duo that the director told the Troffers, "We want to extend your contract another seven weeks."

Terry begged off graciously. "I wish we could, but we already signed a contract for another engagement that begins right after we complete our ten-day engagement with you."

"How long are you booked with them?"

"Two days," said Delilah. "But then we could come back here for the next six weeks and five days, which means we'd start two days late for you."

"Cancel them and stay on with us. Tell them you can't make it."

Terry shook his head. "It's not our policy to cancel out our contracts; we wouldn't lie like that."

"Okay," said the director, who produced contracts for the seven-week engagement. "You'll be here as soon as your two-day engagement is done, right?"

The Troffers reassured him and signed the contract.

Two weeks later, Delilah and Terry received a letter stating that the contract with Circus-Plus for the seven-week engagement was nullified because they didn't cancel out the two-day contract. "But we told them that," said Delilah, frustrated.

"I'm angry enough to go back there," replied Terry. And although they were more than 200 miles away from Circus-Plus's location, the Troffers did drive back to tell the official how upset they were. Even though it didn't change Circus-Plus's decision, it made Terry and Delilah feel better. Having to return to Sarasota with that loss, however, cut deeply into their finances.

Says Delilah, "We lost seven weeks of work. We had to

turn around and go back home and sit idly until the time for the San Juan walk. So we started, very quickly, to fall behind in our bills. Our only consolation was that the San Juan walk would save us from going down the financial drain. Right then and there I learned that once you fall behind it takes years to catch up.

As they watched their savings dwindle, Delilah counted off the days until August on her calendar.

August 16 finally arrived. The Troffer family plus Carol, a friend who would look after the children, arrived in San Juan for Delilah's second skywalk—this one at Hiran Bithorn Stadium.

The promoter picked them up at the airport, rushing around and saying, "You need to hurry. You have to do a promo right away." Too fatigued to move, Delilah acted like a trouper anyway. Shortly thereafter, Carol, a friend of hers, flew in to take care of the children. The five of them were put up at a local hotel close to the stadium.

When the adjoining hotel rooms were found to be missing one bed, the Troffer clan was graciously moved to the Presidential Suite, where there were two bedrooms, two baths, a living room, kitchen, and dining room. Delilah was grateful for the accommodations and that everyone in San Juan who was connected with the walk, including the promoter, treated them superbly, going out of their way to be hospitable.

Offers Delilah, "The only thing that was skewed was the time. They'd tell me, 'We'll pick you up at ten o'clock to do a promo,' but they wouldn't show until eleven or twelve. I started asking if there was something different between American and Puerto Rican time."

Having bought on credit, before leaving America, all the skywalk rigging and equipment they needed, the Troffers were now deeper in debt, which they hoped to erase once

Delilah was paid for her skywalk. She wanted this one to be her biggest success—as it would have been for Vati. For at least six weeks, she had been working out and walking every day with weights to be in the best shape for the San Juan performance. Afterward the promoter had lined up three more skywalks: the next one a month away on September 15, and two more on September 16. So she needed to be strong, determined, and ready.

The morning of her skywalk, Delilah awoke to a brisk, windy day. Looking out the window she shivered, thinking of the wind and how it had pummeled Vati in this same city. She began to get ready, but she knew that soon she'd have to decide whether to go through with the walk. She knew that if it was too windy, she would have to cancel. It was a serious dilemma. If she canceled, she'd look foolish, and they might think she was just afraid because of her grandfather; if she went through with it and shouldn't have, she'd die. "I prayed hard to make the right decision, and as I finished the prayer, all I kept hearing inside my head," explains Delilah, "was 'Step out in faith.' So that's what I did. I went ahead with the walk, stepped out on the wire, and the wind calmed."

During the walk, Delilah and Terry wore earphones so they could communicate. In the middle of the walk, she did a perfect split, and the audience gasped, thinking she was falling. Everyone remembered that her grandfather, the world's best skywalker, had fallen in their city, but their oohs and aahs turned into applause the second they understood what she was doing. It seemed like a long walk to both Delilah and the audience, but when she reached the other end, everyone broke into boisterous cheers and yells. The traffic on the highway running underneath the wire came to a complete stop, horns blared, while drivers and riders got out of their cars clapping. Exhilarated, Delilah understood at last why Vati loved to do the skywalks. Never had she been so proud of her heritage.

That night Delilah slept well, exhausted but proud of herself, in love with her husband and the wire, and eager to collect the much-needed payment, and then walk the wire again. The next morning she told Terry she'd be right back, and headed down the stairs to the hotel clerk to get a morning paper.

"Hello, Miss Wallenda," the clerk bid her in his best English. "You were just wonderful! Everyone loved your walk."

"Thanks," she grinned. "You were there, huh?"

"Oh, no. I laid on the couch and watched you on TV."

Stunned, Delilah stood speechless. She mumbled, "You mean you saw just a bit of it, right? Like a clip of it, a preview?"

"No, no," he said, "I saw your walk from start to finish."

Delilah took a deep breath, politely thanked him for his praise, then returned to the suite to tell Terry, who promptly contacted the promoter.

"In order to get commercial time for the show," responded the promoter, "I sold your walk for $65,000 to the television station."

"You brought us here under the promise that you would honor our contract, and then you went ahead and broke our agreement. Because you showed the walk on television, you have to compensate Delilah."

That night, as scheduled, Delilah repeated her walk—keeping her end of the deal—then she and Terry tore down. But now no one was around to help, no nice people going out of their way to be hospitable, and certainly no promoter anywhere in sight.

The next day they were ready to leave San Juan when the promoter arrived at their hotel, bearing a check with only half the money owed the Troffers.

"It's all I have," he said.

With little hope and little time to argue, Terry said nothing more, but took the check and hopped into a cab. He rushed to a bank to cash the check before the promoter could put a stop on it. Less than an hour later he returned to the hotel lobby where Delilah, the children, and her friend Carol waited.

Just by his expression, Delilah knew something was wrong.

"What is it?" she asked.

He shook his head and said, "The bank won't cash it; they say he doesn't have that kind of money."

"We left San Juan penniless," Delilah says sighing. "The only money we had on us was $100, which about paid for our cab fare. And to think of all the expense we went to just to do that walk."

At the airport, the Troffers were quiet, each lost to their own thoughts. Terry glanced at his wife, who had risked her life for that skywalk, and he said, "You're not going to cry, are you?"

She said, "Of course not," and broke down and sobbed.

They knew suing the promoter wasn't the answer. San Juan's constitution was different from American laws, and what good was it anyway to "wring a cloth dry that's already dry to begin with?" the Troffers decided. Still, their own bankruptcy loomed as a larger possibility than ever. At home in the States, Delilah looked back on her San Juan experience and realized it had been a bad trip for both her and Vati. Could things get much worse? she wondered.

A few days later Delilah got word that her cousin Ricky had fallen from the wire at Shrine Circus and was badly hurt. Despite their estrangement, she immediately called the hospital. "I only got to talk to his wife Debbie, but Terry and I offered to help by taking down his rigging and taking care of their child. They declined, but I telephoned one more time and this time talked to Ricky and wished him well," says Delilah.

A call came in to the Troffers asking if they'd do Ricky's October dates. Ironically, it was the agent who had earlier refused Terry's bid to do those same dates because his was higher; instead, he had hired Ricky. But the Troffers agreed to do the engagement for Ricky without asking what the fee was: they told the agent they'd accept whatever Ricky's contract had called for.

After this, however, jobs became scarcer.

As time went on, although Delilah was steadily becoming a world-wide skywalk sensation, her finances were rapidly plummeting. Meanwhile the Wallenda family was fighting again. Helen's side of the family was sending scathing letters to different influential people in the circus business contending that Jenny was creating problems in the Wallenda family by lying and making public family business. Jenny chose not to dignify any comment by responding. Delilah consoled her mother and turned to more pressing problems.

Being out of work now for five-and-a-half months was the major thing she worried about. The only date she and Terry had been able to line up so far was a run at Jolly Rogers in Ocean City, Maryland, from Memorial Day to Labor Day. From there, they'd move on to Atlantic City, New Jersey, to do a ten-day fair. That was it. Their money situation got uglier each day. Sometimes Delilah felt as though she'd shatter into a thousand pieces. They even started to think about leaving Sarasota—leaving family, friends, their house —to live further up north in Florida where the cost-of-living was less. For one thing, the taxes on their house had doubled since they had purchased it. Delilah hoped against hope that things would start getting better, but the summer ended with their bills piling up even higher.

Delilah took a job with Terry's dad cleaning the windows of the buildings the men had waterproofed. In between, Terry and Delilah worked on getting bookings for the next season. Only one-day spots were offered, but the Troffers accepted every one of them gratefully.

Meanwhile the situation within the two sides of the Wallenda family had deteriorated even further. Ugly rumors about Ricky and Delilah's having a court fight circulated. Promoters no longer wanted to hire the Troffers because they were fearful of being taken to court by Ricky, who was still claiming that Delilah was not a real Wallenda. To Delilah, who was mortified, it seemed as though employers everywhere were questioning her heredity. Her employability drastically dropped. But in spite of this, her main concern was Terry, because he was not feeling any better.

At the Tennessee State Fair in Nashville, she watched her husband hammer iron stakes into the ground to anchor the rigging. Suddenly Terry squatted on the ground, moaning, "I'm dizzy." Because it didn't happen to him again for the rest of the Tennessee engagement, Terry thought it was nothing more than a loss of equilibrium after having stopped for so long. But during the successive autumn months, he experienced additional dizzy spells accompanied by a hearing loss in his left ear. Soon he was back on the doctor rounds again.

The first doctor told him, "See an ear, nose, and throat specialist."

Terry did.

The second doctor—a specialist—ran a battery of tests and came back looking grim. "Looks like you have Meniere's Disease. There's no cure. You'll eventually go deaf, so you'd better quit the highwire."

Terry felt frustrated. *Sure, Doc,* he thought, *why don't you give up practicing medicine after all those years of hard work? Just get up and walk away from it. Let your family go bankrupt.* But what he said aloud was, "I'd like to get a second opinion."

He got an appointment with a top specialist in Tampa who ran another series of tests. "Maybe it's a brain tumor; the MRI scan is inconclusive. I can't say for sure what it is. Keep a journal of your spells and report them to me. If it's Meniere's, we might as well get you started on medication."

Eventually the medication worked; the dizzy spells grew less and less frequent until they almost disappeared.

Terry felt more confident about walking the wire. But then the dizziness happened again. One night Delilah was standing on Terry's shoulders when suddenly a spell slammed into him. "Hold on honey," he cried out as he aimed for the platform, his arms hugging the railing. They made it, but Terry knew he was still sick. "Wait for me by the rigging," he told her.

When he made it down the ladder, he took a bow with one hand while grasping the ladder with the other. The audience watched as he lovingly threw his arm around Delilah, not knowing she was holding him up as they walked back to the dressing room.

Coping with Terry's illness and their financial woes was difficult enough, but even more wrenching was Ricky and Delilah's continuous battle which now reached the critical stage. Delilah, who would have rather been working with her cousin than fighting with him, wondered what had happened to the camaraderie all the Wallendas, and especially she and Ricky, had once enjoyed.

What angered Jenny's side of the family more than anything was Ricky's claim that Delilah was not a Wallenda and shouldn't use that name; yet, he gave it away to others who were in no way related to any Wallenda. An example appeared in one of his newsletters, in which he wrote, "I guess I forgot to mention the direction of Philip 'Greek' Gikas Wallenda." To this, Jenny comments, "Ricky just gave this fellow our last name, and I believe the man only worked for my Dad just before he died. The 'Greek' was one of the men who set up the skywalk for my dad in San Juan the day he fell." Delilah was saddened that Ricky could give Philip the name of Wallenda when he had been with Vati for such a short time, and yet Ricky denied Delilah, who was entitled to the name, the right to use it.

Rather than making trouble, however, Delilah went on with her own life, hoping justice would win out in the end. She concentrated on Terry, who kept on having one health problem after another. One day while working for his father, Terry injured his back, forcing him to go to a doctor, who told him he'd have to do therapy twice a week and not work for three months. Delilah agonized, not believing how badly things were going in her life.

April arrived, and while working one of the few dates they had, Terry injured his foot en route to the Shrine Circus booking in Nashville; somehow he managed to get through the engagement.

When finished with their Nashville date they started driving home, but with Terry not feeling well, they decided to lay-over at a campground. Early in the morning he woke his wife. "Oh, my side. I can't stand the pain," he told her.

She shuddered. Now what could it be? And his side? When had his side started bothering him? She took him to the nearest hospital, where he was diagnosed as having a kidney stone. They returned to Sarasota, hoping things would improve.

The only bright note came right before the end of the year. Their daughter Lijana, then fourteen years old, approached Delilah. "Mom," she said, "I want to walk the wire just like you."

With tears of pride glistening in her eyes, Delilah stared at her child for a long minute. Despite Delilah's pride in Lijana following the Wallenda heritage, Delilah wondered whether it was right to encourage this girl to take up a career in a business that was on the decline? Should she steer her to something more promising, more secure? "Well, Lijana," began Delilah, the words of her grandfather echoing in her ears, "If you really want it, you have to prove it to me."

Lijana practiced hard every day, even when she thought her mother wasn't looking.

EPILOGUE

It is May of 1992, and Terry and Delilah foresee another bleak summer in the making. They wonder, "What has happened to all the circus jobs?" Because of the bad state of the business, Delilah became even more cautious about encouraging her children, even Lijana, to enter her trade. She tells them to concentrate on their studies. Staying at home, waiting for the almost always silent phone to ring, reinforces her belief that Nikolas and Lijana need an education in order to be whatever they hope to become in life.

"If it happens that they want to follow in my footsteps," says Delilah, "I won't stop them, because circus life—performing—is in our blood. The Wallendas have been performers for generations. But I won't fixate them on the idea, either, and I won't be at all disappointed if they choose a different lifestyle or go into conventional careers." She lovingly glances at her daughter.

Then Delilah adds, "Even though she already shows all the talent of a Wallenda, I'm not saying anything to her either way about her interest in walking the highwire. Time will tell." But Delilah smiles when she adds that Lijana recently did her first public wirewalk act in May at Patlaka, Florida, while Nikolas served as the announcer. Delilah and her daughter made their costumes. It's this family unity that Delilah enjoys most, whether they're at home practicing the wire in their backyard or on the road, moving from one location to the next.

However, Delilah is saddened that some of the family's estranged relationships are still fraught with friction and others are passing away.

In mid-June, J.Y., Delilah's step-grandfather, dies. Says Delilah, "He left me his little donkey. I remember how I used to call him every Sunday, even when we were on the road. Sometimes I forget he's gone and I go to the phone to call him." J.Y. was eighty-four.

A few days afterward, the Troffers feel it necessary to have their attorney seek injunction relief from her cousin Ricky's allegations.

While the Troffers await Ricky's reaction to the injunction being filed, a reporter gets word of the suit and writes an article on it for the July 20th *Sarasota Herald-Tribune*, entitled "Wallenda Files Suit Against Cousin":

> Two members of one of America's most famous circus families could go from high wire to the courtroom, with one cousin accusing another of spreading rumors that she's not an "authentic Wallenda." . . . She asks that a judge enjoin him from such statements. . . . The lawsuit says he told the publisher and author of a book about her life that she's not an "authentic Wallenda."[33]

The legal machinations continue as the cousins who were once so close battle one another for what each believes is his or her own entitlement. With the injunction filed, they hit an impasse.

Finally both parties agree to settle out of court. Both acknowledge "that Delilah Wallenda Troffer is the natural granddaughter of Karl and Martha Wallenda and, as such, rightfully performs as a Wallenda, using the Wallenda name." They also acknowledge "that Enrico Wallenda is the natural grandson of Karl and Martha Wallenda, two of the four original members of the Great Wallenda Highwire Troupe which first performed in the United States of America, also consisting of Herman Wallenda and Joseph Geiger."

Meanwhile, the rest of Delilah's part of the family spin out their destiny.

Delilah's half-sister Tammy has taken fate into her own hands: at sixteen she left home, at seventeen she had a baby, at eighteen she divorced, but remained in show business. She assumed the stage name of Tamara and has left the highwire to train wild animals. She says it took months for her to work up the nerve to tell her mom and dad—Jenny and Andy—that she no longer wanted to be on the wire. Her parents are not happy with that decision; she says in an AP article: "My parents felt so safe fifty feet up in the air, and then my mother screams at me to be careful with the cats." Tamara's five-year-old daughter is already interested in following in her mother's footsteps.

Delilah's brother Tino, his wife Olinka, and their children remain in Sarasota near Delilah, and like the Troffers they too pray for continued work, as well as direction and guidance. They still work on the wire, and Tino also produces Circus Moran throughout the year.

Gunther Wallenda, who's retired from teaching, enjoys his

time at home with his wife Sheila. He kindly entertains reporters' questions, but he seldom calls attention to his life as a former "Great Wallenda." He's proud of his accomplishments since the "seven-man" fall. At sixty-five, Gunther looks back on the past as just that—the past; he feels he gave all of himself to it at the time. He walked away from the highwire and his teaching with a feeling of satisfaction because he knows, as does everyone else, that he's a man of courage.

Mario Wallenda, still wheelchair-bound, has been married to Linda for thirty years. Of their time together, Linda says, "I've managed to tip over his wheelchair a few times and spill him out." But even after the "seven-man" fell and spilled him out, he's been able to pick himself up and go on with his life, and a productive one at that. Not only does he work as an inspector for Bausch and Lomb contact lenses, but he has since the accident completed high school and taken college-level courses. He looks back and reflects on his past with pride. The dissension in the family bothers him but does not occupy him; he lives life as fully as he can and harbors no resentment for what the past has done to his future. "I still miss the circus," Mario offers. "I miss the traveling, the excitement, and the friends. Today, though, I don't know anyone in the business. The faces have changed." Solemnly, he adds, "Circuses are so expensive today, I don't know how anyone can afford to go, and maybe that's why they're dying. I am shocked at the prices for popcorn and admissions. Still, I think the business will always be around . . . just not in the same form it is today. For one thing, the present emphasis is on sex and theatrics. When I was performing, it was strictly on artistry and skill."

Jenny Wallenda has become the unofficial matriarch of her part of the family. Always she feels part of the Great

Wallenda Tradition. She has given 100 percent of herself to the business, her children, and her relatives. Like a mother bear, she keeps her ears peeled and eyes fixed on her children and grandchildren, as well as her cousin Gunther and brother Mario, as she knows what pain each has gone through. And although she too has experienced heartache, she's reticent to speak about it. Proud to be Karl's older child, she is equally proud of what she's done since her father's death. For her, as for him, the show must go on. So she is forever dipping her hand into the circus bucket and coming up with something she can help with, whether it's putting on a parade or producing a show. Over the years, she and Delilah have drawn closer together, appreciating both the joys and the sorrows they have shared in the past and looking forward to continuing to share in the future. Still, for Jenny, it is not the same as it was before the awful but famed accident. A *Sarasota Herald-Tribune* article of November 19, 1986, summed it up best:

> Jenny Wallenda Anderson remembered when being a Wallenda meant you were more than a circus performer; you were a dignitary. "For years we were ambassadors from Sarasota," she said. "Everywhere we went we advertised (it) was little in those days and we (the Wallendas) were big. We helped put (it) on the map."

Now retired and home, Jenny looks after her husband Andy, who's been ill. Sometimes she feels dispirited being in the middle of the intense family feud—quite a change for a woman who took the world by storm, sitting atop the seven-man in a wobbling chair as the pyramid's top-mounter. She too senses that she has toppled from that lofty position; however, Jenny has accepted with grace the fact that her retirement, her settling in, is Delilah's beginning.

"And some day soon, my daughter Lijana will be picking up where I've left off," says Delilah.

At this writing, Terry is still contending with his Meniere's disease, though the disorder is under control and he's finally able to climb the wire and work.

Offers Delilah, "The medicine he takes helps a lot, so he's doing much better and not even having dizzy spells now."

Because jobs in the circus are so scarce, the Troffers split their time between working for Terry's father, and their real mission, working the wire.

Delilah continues, "I worry about the end of the circus, because I think it could be around the corner. The cut-throat competition in the business, coupled with all the problems the Troffers have experienced, might cause less courageous people to give up, but they do not."

Meanwhile, Terry and Delilah's summer work schedule looks meager: July 1–4 they're scheduled to do an engagement in Cincinnati; August 12–17, they'll be in Harrisonburg, Virginia, for a booking, and then they'll do another date in Pittsburgh from August 30 to September 2—all of which adds up to less than thirty days of employment for the entire season. These hardships are reflective of their life, and yet, because of their faith, Delilah doesn't feel depressed. "I don't pity myself, I look ahead and trust God," she says, standing tall with her head high.

And so, she keeps pushing on, never giving up, struggling to be the best of her profession and always doing her best to be a good wife and mother. Boldly she skywalks and performs on the highwire, making inroads in places where others have failed, including her own renowned grandfather. Her goal of saving the circus is always in her mind.

And while Vati moved from life to death, Delilah moves counter—from his death to life, keeping her balance, walking forward, focusing on victory.

NOTES

1. Portions of this chapter appeared in a different form in *Signs of the Times* magazine, 1991.
2. Duvall's comments were made before the demise of communism and the breakup of the Soviet Union.
3. Much of the old family history comes from Ron Morris's *Karl Wallenda* (Chatham, NY: Sagarin Press, 1976).
4. As told to Mary Jane Miller, *The Sarasota Citizen*, August 6, 1964, p. 12.
5. Ibid.
6. Morris, *Karl Wallenda*, p. 148.
7. Ibid., p. 149.
8. Ibid., p. 153.
9. *Mutti*, from the German for "mother," is a term given to grandmothers. Likewise, Karl Wallenda's nickname *Vati* is from the German for "father."
10. Morris, *Karl Wallenda*, p. 161. The Wallendas claim no knowledge of how Dieter really escaped.
11. From the NBC television movie "The Great Wallendas."
12. Gilbert Millstein, "Why They Walk the Wire," *The New York Times Magazine*, February 1962, p. 28.
13. Morris, *Karl Wallenda*.

14. Ibid.
15. Ibid.
16. Ibid.
17. Ibid.
18. "The Great Wallendas."
19. Ibid.
20. Ibid.
21. Morris, *Karl Wallenda*.
22. Ibid.
23. Ibid.
24. From the DuPont documentary "A Walk in the Sun."
25. Morris, *Karl Wallenda*, p. 182.
26. Paul Hemphill, "Hey, Mr. Wallenda, You Gonna Do That Dangerous One Tonight?" *Today's Health*, June 1973, p. 46.
27. Ibid.
28. David Grimes, "The Wallenda Family Maintains a Steady Balance," *The Sarasota Herald-Tribune*, November 19, 1986, p. 2TMC.
29. Ibid.
30. Ibid.
31. *Currents* magazine, August 19, 1981.
32. The name of this circus has been changed.
33. Laura Higgins, "Wallenda Files Suit Against Cousin," *The Sarasota Herald-Tribune*, July 20, 1992.